T0006315

EDINBURGH

Like a Local

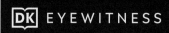

EDINBURGH
Like a Local

BY THE PEOPLE WHO CALL IT HOME

Contents

EAT

DRINK

SHOP

ARTS & CULTURE

NIGHTLIFE

OUTDOORS

meet the locals

KENZA MARLAND

Arts journalist Kenza has lived, worked and studied in Edinburgh for over a decade. When she's not writing, she's galloping over Edinburgh's seven hills, eating out and going to gigs.

MICHAEL CLARK

Edinburgh native Michael has lived in London for five years, but he misses his old haunts in Auld Reekie. Editor by day, he spends his time writing, recording and channelling his inner diva under the moniker "clarq".

STUART KENNY

Travel writer and spoken word artist Stuart has lived in Edinburgh for 25 years. He's happiest when mountain biking, performing in basement bookshops or chilling with a beer in hand – locally brewed of course.

XANDRA ROBINSON-BURNS

Xandra moved to the city for the theatre, walks and to write in coffee shops. She chronicles her everyday life on www.heroinetraining.com, where she encourages us all to find the wonder in our everyday lives.

Edinburgh

WELCOME TO THE CITY

Edinburgh folk are a wonderfully mixed bag. They're salt-of-the-earth working-class Scots, hard-grafting creatives and slick-suited professionals. They're free-spirited hippies, students from around the world and old dears who've lived on the same street their entire lives. And uniting them all? A shared sense of pride in the captivating city they call home.

Right enough, if ever there were a city to capture your heart, it's Edinburgh. Its mesmerizing maze of cobbled closes and enchanting architecture has inspired countless artists, writers and creatives over the years. Oh, and speaking of the arts, every summer the city hosts the biggest arts festival in the world, with millions rocking up for a slice of the action. The locals might feign annoyance, but they're the ones chanting "one more tune" as the party draws to a close.

It's not all festivals and frolics though. This city has seen its fair share of tough times. Sure, *Trainspotting* was fiction,

but it was grounded in truth – scratch just below the surface and you'll see that some of these issues are still prevalent today. Yet Edinburgh is, above all, a caring place. The locals support each other through thick and thin. And while fiercely loyal to their own communities, they welcome the new with warm hearts, open minds and a wee dash of that cutting Scots wit (just to keep you on your toes, mind).

They're also an opinionated bunch, and that's where this book comes in. We know the places that locals adore, from indie art galleries to bars masquerading as barbershops. Of course, these pages can't capture every local's experience, but instead offer a snapshot of city life.

So whether you're a local looking to unearth your city's secrets, or you're keen to discover something new, this book will help you to embrace Edinburgh with the fun-loving spirit for which it's known. Enjoy Edinburgh, but do it the local way.

Liked by the locals

"Edinburgh has welcomed me
as one of its own. There's really
nowhere quite like it. With its
winding cobbled streets and huge,
spectacular skies, it's a place
people find incredibly hard to
leave. Like most, I've fallen in
love with it. You will too."

KENZA MARLAND, ARTS JOURNALIST AND COPYWRITER

Seasons matter in Edinburgh. As they change, the city swings from winter warmers huddled in the pub to BBQ smoke-filled summer afternoons.

Edinburgh
THROUGH THE YEAR

SPRING

BEER GARDENS

After a long, dark winter, grabbing a pint in the sunshine couldn't be more of a treat. At the first glimpse of sun, locals rush to fill beer gardens city-wide.

NATURE WALKS

Locals embrace the spring weather with walks along the canal or Water of Leith, made all the more pleasant by the arrival of cute ducklings and spring blossoms.

MARKETS GALORE

Street food markets are the best place to sample the wares of local sellers. With options including Leith Farmers' Market, Stockbridge Market and The Pitt, locals are spoilt for choice.

SLÁINTE

May is Whisky Month in Scotland, and locals raise a glass (or two) at whisky-themed events all over the city.

SUMMER

FESTIVAL FROLICS

For the entirety of August the city hosts the Edinburgh International Festival, the biggest arts festival in the world. Inundated with performers and good-timers, the place becomes a circus of fireworks, frolics and festivities.

SEA SWIMS

Summer brings with it trips to Portobello beach, wanders out to Cramond Island and adventures along the east coast to North Berwick, ice cream in hand.

TAPS AFF

On rare scorchers, folk make a beeline for the city's green spaces. Clothes come off at alarming speed, and many a local lad will strut around "taps aff" on a hot (or even moderately sunny) day.

LATE LIGHT NIGHTS

Locals really make the most of the extended daylight hours during summer. And with clubs open till 5am in August, the city seems to forgo sleep entirely.

AUTUMN

FIRESIDE PINTS

As the nights draw in, Edinburgh's pubs fill with animated punters insisting on another round by the open hearth.

CULTURE LIVE

The summer festivals are a tough act to follow, but in autumn the show must go on. Evenings are spent in packed-out theatres and performance venues.

RAINY-DAY ACTIVITIES

Driech days are spent inside the city's many art galleries and museums, where locals lose themselves in a maze of exhibits long after the rain has stopped.

HALLOWEEN HAPPENINGS

Halloween, Bonfire Night and the Celtic Samhuinn Fire Festival: Edinburgh goes all out for spooky celebrations (this city is said to be seriously haunted after all).

WINTER

CHRISTMAS IN THE CITY

Princes Street Gardens are filled with folks sipping mulled wine and buying gingerbread and spicy *Currywurst* while waiting for their go on the Big Wheel.

SNOWY ADVENTURES

Most winters bring at least some snow. And when it finally arrives, locals hurtle themselves downhill on sledges, oven trays and other improvised alternatives.

HOGMANAY

Revellers gather in their thousands to see in the new year at the biggest street party of their lives. Fireworks illuminate the streets and the crowd sings "Auld Lang Syne" while sharing a dram.

THE LOONY DOOK

Hardy souls blow away the cobwebs with a bracing New Year's Day dip in the chilly waters of the North Sea.

There's an art to being an Edinburger, from the dos and don'ts in the pub to negotiating the city's intricate streets. Here's a breakdown of all you need to know.

Edinburgh
KNOW-HOW

For a directory of health and safety resources, safe spaces, and accessibility information, turn to page 190. For everything else, read on.

EAT
Edinburgh folk will find any excuse to eat out. Cafés start to buzz from around 11am – if you arrive any later, prepare to queue. On-the-go options include greasy spoons, bakeries and delis, but dinner (eaten between 6pm and 10pm) is a sacred sit-down affair. During the week you can usually rock up unannounced (unless you're headed somewhere fancy), but it's best to book ahead at the weekends, when places are busy.

DRINK
Pub culture is big business here. Pubs usually open from around 12pm but, while day drinking is a thing, Scots tend to save the serious session for after dinner. The culture of a "round" – buying drinks for your group, which each person reciprocates – is an unspoken rule. Last orders are usually called at around 11:30pm Monday to Thursday, a bit later on Friday and Saturday, and 11pm on Sundays, always followed by a half-hour "drinking-up time".

SHOP
Shopping in Edinburgh is divided by area. George Street is for designer names, Princes Street for affordable fashion and the Old Town for artisan goods. It's pretty easy to spot the authentic shops amid tourist traps selling towel kilts , and the city's independents really do appreciate your business. Shops are generally open 9am–6pm daily, but many stay open later on Thursdays. Oh, and plastic bags cost 10p each, so carry a tote.

ARTS & CULTURE

Many museums and galleries are free – something that the locals make full use of. That said, small, independent museums tend to cost a little to enter, but never a lot. Theatre tickets are also reasonable, especially in festival season. Locals don't tend to dress up for an evening show, but anything goes. And speaking of the Festival, if you're on a budget, hit up the Free Fringe and pay what you like for hit (and miss) comedy. Locals read *The List* and *The Skinny* to find out what's on throughout the year. *www.freefringe.org.uk*

NIGHTLIFE

Bars tend to open in the afternoon until 1am and clubs until 3am, though licences are extended for the Festival and over Christmas and New Year (to 3am and 5am respectively). If you're out in the New Town, dress up; for the Old Town or Leith, stay casual. Wherever you go, always carry ID as proof of age. Chippies and kebab shops shut at 1am, so get your late-night scran in before then.

OUTDOORS

One thing you can't rely on here is the weather, so always be prepared for four seasons in one day. If the sun shines, locals will grab a few "tinnies" and head to the nearest park. The Meadows is the city's go-to picnic spot – be sure you bin your litter when you leave. The leafy paths of the old railway network make for a lovely stroll but note walkers share the narrow paths with cyclists.

Keep in mind

Here are some tips and tidbits that will help you fit in like a local.

» **Card vs cash** The majority of places accept contactless payments, but it's always worth carrying a small amount of cash.

» **No smoking** Smoking is banned in public places in Scotland. If you must smoke, do it in a designated area outside and don't drop butts.

» **Tip if you like** It's polite to tip waiters and table-service bartenders (around 10 per cent) and taxi drivers (to the nearest pound), but it's not expected.

» **Stay hydrated** Plenty of cafés and restaurants are happy to refill your water bottle – just ask nicely.

GETTING AROUND

Edinburgh is a small city, made up of
a series of neighbourhoods *(p14)*, some
consisting of only a few streets at most.
Its compact size makes it easy to get
around. Most of the action takes place
in the Old Town or the New Town, which
are linked by North Bridge, Waverley
Bridge and the Mound. Locals tend to
navigate by the position of the sea to the
north and east, the Pentland Hills to the
south and the castle in the centre. Areas
are grouped into postcodes ranging
from EH1 (which encompasses the Old
Town) up to EH17, further out of town.

To keep you right, we've provided
what3words addresses for each sight
in this book, meaning you can quickly
pinpoint exactly where you're heading.

On foot

In a city as perfectly small as Edinburgh,
walking is by far the best way to see it in
all its glory – take your time and you'll
discover some cool shortcuts, amazing
architecture and stunning views. Plus
you'll be helping the environment (and
avoiding the traffic) as you stroll. Step
away from the main drag if you need to
stop to take photos or check directions,
as the locals like to move fast. And if
they're disgruntled, they're not shy
about letting you know.

On wheels

The hills and potholes of Edinburgh
aren't exactly a cyclist's dream, but the
city's cycling infrastructure is getting
better. The city centre is becoming
increasingly car-free, and there are
marked bike lanes on main routes (be
careful when cycling over tram tracks),
with traffic lights now featuring an early
green light for cyclists. Despite these
improvements, most locals bypass the
roads entirely and get from A to B via
the Water of Leith Walkway. This old
railway network now forms a series of
paths for both walkers and cyclists.

Edinburgh's shared-bike scheme is
ideal for visitors. You'll need to download
the app and make your way to one of
the many docking stations. From here
it's £1.50 for a single trip and £3 for a
multi-pass trip that lasts 24 hours. For
longer periods, hire a bike from one of
many central bike shops; Biketrax and
the Edinburgh Bicycle Co-op are both
great options.
www.edinburghcyclehire.com

By public transport

Edinburgh doesn't have a metro or an
underground, but it does have a tram
system that's being extended all the
way from the airport to Leith (don't get
locals started on that one: the constant

roadworks have been a nuisance since construction began in 2008). Even so, most residents are happy to stick with the bus. Lothian Buses go more or less everywhere in the city. It's £1.80 for a single or £4.50 for a day ticket and all fares are payable as soon as you step on board, by cash (you need exact change) or contactless. Prices go up after midnight and the service itself is reduced at night. Another bus service, First Bus, will take you out of the city to surrounding areas but, for day trips, the train rules. ScotRail operates an excellent network across the country with affordable off-peak tickets. *www.scotrail.co.uk*

By car or taxi

Edinburgh can be a frustrating city to drive around, with roadworks, one-way systems and limited parking. Locals prefer to walk or bike around, but taxis are a great shout for an evening out. You can hail down a black cab any time one passes, so long as it has its orange light illuminated, or queue for a lift at one of many taxi ranks dotted around the centre of town. Most locals opt for a slightly cheaper private taxi company – Central Taxis or Capital Cars are both reliable options. There's always the ubiquitous Uber, too.

Download these

We recommend you download these apps to help you get about the city.

WHAT3WORDS
Your geocoding friend
A what3words address is a simple way to communicate any precise location on earth, using just three words. ///proof.trails.penny, for example, is the code for Lighthouse Books' entrance on West Nicholson Street. Simply download the free what3words app, type a what3words address into the search bar, and you'll know exactly where to go.

TRANSPORT FOR EDINBURGH
Your local transport service
The app from Lothian Buses provides live travel times for bus and tram services, tells you where the nearest stop is, and tracks when the bus or tram will be arriving in real time. It's a great source for checking when the last bus or tram is, too, so you don't miss either.

Edinburgh feels more like a collection of villages than a capital city, and each has its own distinct vibe. Here we take a look at some of our favourites.

Edinburgh
NEIGHBOURHOODS

Abbeyhill and Easter Road

Long-standing residents have called this place home for generations, but the city's young professionals have finally got wind of its charms (and affordability). Making the most of these newcomers are a flurry of cafés and indie businesses setting up shop next door to Easter Road's oldest boozers. *{map 3}*

Broughton

Skirting the fringes of Edinburgh's "Pink Triangle" of LGBTQ+ bars, bohemian Broughton has a lot going for it. The area's restaurants and laidback pubs are an extension of the home, and residents are devout in their support. *{map 3}*

Bruntsfield

Bottomless brunch spots, artisan bakeries, yoga studios and pristine shopfronts that glimmer in the sunlight. If the opposite of nightlife is day life, Bruntsfield has it by the barrowload. *{map 5}*

Canonmills

Best known for the Botanic Gardens, leafy Canonmills is home to wholesome young families, senior citizens and an adorable pair of otters who you might just spot splashing around in the Water of Leith. *{map 3}*

Cowgate

Unassuming by day, the city's gritty underbelly comes alive at night when the roads are closed to give punters plenty of space to make their way from pub to club. Back in the day, the Cowgate was a warren of mischief and revelry, and not much has changed since. *{map 1}*

Dean Village

This former mill town is where every local wants to live. Some do, but most visit on a peaceful walk from Stockbridge or the West End. *{map 2}*

Gorgie and Dalry

In Victorian times this area was a hotbed of industry. The factories have since closed, but the familiar hoppy aroma of the Fountain Brewery is a reminder of the area's past. *{map 6}*

Holyrood

Old meets new in Holyrood. There's the palace, the uber-modern Parliament Building (residents still can't decide whether they like it or loathe it), and, oh yeah, an extinct volcano. {map 3}

Leith

Leith isn't up and coming: it's well and truly up. Gone is the gritty reputation from *Trainspotting*; youngsters are making the most of cheap rents, cute pubs and fancy restaurants. Leith was a town in its own right until 1920, and the community spirit still burns strong. {map 4}

Morningside

Its wide-set avenues may be lined with the city's swankiest houses, but Morningside is also home to a neighbourly community who look out for one another. {map 5}

New Town

There's no denying it, the New Town (which is still pretty old, by the way) is posh. George Street is the spot for luxury brands, elegant bars and exclusive clubs. Set back

a few blocks are Georgian townhouses, gridded streets and leafy circuses. {map 2}

Old Town

A medieval maze of cobbled streets and hidden closes, this place is tourist central. The souvenir shops, bag-pipers and ghost tours are a bit much for most locals, but even the Royal Mile has some local haunts, and folk here have a soft spot for its tartan-touting charm. {map 1}

Portobello

When locals want to escape the city, they retreat to this former Victorian resort town for some sea air. As well as a gorgeous sandy beach, there are plenty of shops, cafés, pubs and restaurants. {map 6}

Southside

From the sprawling green space of the Meadows to the charmingly chaotic international food stores of Nicolson Street, the Southside is a smorgasbord of cultures and moods. A young crowd brings a fresh energy and, during the

Festival, the area bursts into life with pop-up shows and street food stalls. {map 5}

Stockbridge

Once a village on the outskirts, Stockbridge is now a trendy neighbourhood just a stone's throw from the city centre. It's retained its village vibe, with a quaint high street lined with local shops and young families pushing prams around the weekly farmers' market. {map 2}

Tollcross

Always busy, and a wee bit brash, Tollcross is all about big entertainment venues, music halls, classic boozers and modern offices. There's a buzz about the place, with theatre-goers hitting up bars for a pre- and post-performance pint. {map 2}

West End

Elegant streets, high-end boutiques and fancy wine bars are ten a penny in the well-to-do West End. Served by Haymarket Station, the area is also a rush hour hub for commuters heading in and out of town. {map 2}

Edinburgh
ON THE MAP

Whether you're looking for your new favourite spot or want to check out what each part of Edinburgh has to offer, our maps – along with handy map references throughout the book – have you covered.

ROSYTH

M90

SOUTH QUEENSFERRY

A90

M90

M9

KIRKLISTON

M9

Edinburg Airport

A89

BROXBURN

M8

RATHO

A71

A89

DEANS

LADYWELL

BATHGATE

M8

EAST CALDER

A70

LIVINGSTON

A71

BLACKBURN

A704

WEST CALDER

A70

| 0 kilometres | 3 |
| 0 miles | 3 |

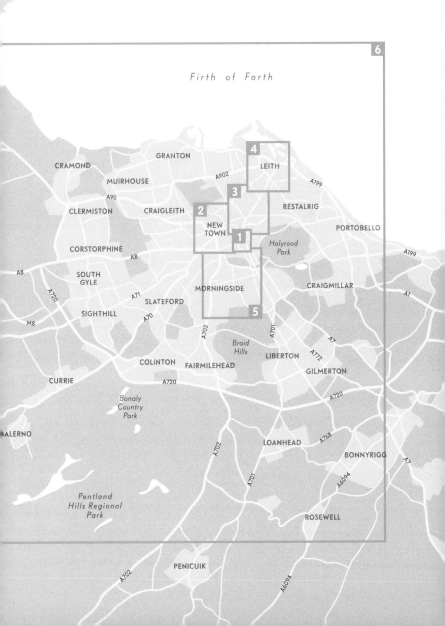

ALGETY BAY

Firth of Forth

6

CRAMOND

GRANTON

4

LEITH

A902

MUIRHOUSE

3

A90

CRAIGLEITH

2

CLERMISTON

RESTALRIG

NEW
TOWN

1

CORSTORPHINE

A8

PORTOBELLO

*Holyrood
Park*

A199

SOUTH
GYLE

A71

MORNINGSIDE

CRAIGMILLAR

A1

SLATEFORD

5

SIGHTHILL

A70

A701

A702

*Braid
Hills*

LIBERTON

A772

A7

COLINTON

FAIRMILEHEAD

A720

GILMERTON

CURRIE

A720

A702

*Bonaly
Country
Park*

LOANHEAD

A768

BALERNO

A702

BONNYRIGG

A7

A701

A6094

*Pentland
Hills Regional
Park*

ROSEWELL

A702

PENICUIK

A6094

0 metres 100
0 yards 100

WAVERLEY BRIDGE

Edinburgh Waverley Station

NORTH BRIDGE

MARKET STREET

Fruitmarket Gallery A

EAST MARKET STREET

JEFFREY STREET

A Scotsman Picturehouse

Ecco Vino
Underground Solu'shn S D A Stills

COCKBURN STREET

MARKET STREET

The Devil's Advocate D

Arcade Haggis E
and Whisky House

Museum of Childhood A

NORTH BANK ST

Royal Mile O

HIGH STREET

Whistle N Binkies

BLACKFRIARS ST

N Edinburgh Larder

The Writers' A Museum

St Giles' Cathedral

BANK ST

HUNTER SQUARE

Department of Magic: N Prophecies Quest

BLAIR STREET

The Banshee N Labyrinth

LAWNMARKET

GEORGE IV BRIDGE

OLD TOWN

Wings N

City Café E

SOUTH BRIDGE

COWGATE

Walker S Slater

I.J. Mellis S

VICTORIA STREET

Cabaret Voltaire E

N Bannerman's

The Red Door Gallery

N The Liquid Room

Stramash N N La Belle Angele
The Mash House N

The Bongo N Club

N Sneaky Pete's

The Jazz Bar N

N The Royal Oak

COWGATE

E The Outsider

D Under the Stairs

CHAMBERS STREET

Armstrongs S Vintage

CANDLEMAKER ROW

Little Blue S Door Vintage

Brass Monkey A

Captain's Bar N

National Museum A of Scotland

Greyfriars Kirk

Sandy Bell's N

FORREST ROAD

A Bedlam Theatre

N Paradise Palms

POTTERROW

Festival A Theatre

A Surgeons' Hall Museum

SOUTHSIDE

NICOLSON SQUARE

Ting Thai E Caravan

BRISTO SQUARE

Mosque E Kitchen

CHAPEL STREET

LAURISTON PLACE

E Tupiniquim

TEVIOT PLACE

MIDDLE MEADOW WALK

Edinburgh University

CHARLES ST

A Anatomical Museum

MAP 1

1

The Cocktail
Geeks

HIGH STREET

ST. MARY'S STREET

COWGATE

Dovecot
Studios

DRUMMOND STREET

RICHMOND

PLACE

NICOLSON STREET

🄴 EAT

Arcade Haggis and
    Whisky House *(p41)*
City Café *(p35)*
Edinburgh Larder *(p33)*
Mosque Kitchen *(p43)*
The Outsider *(p37)*
Ting Thai Caravan *(p50)*
Tupiniquim *(p36)*

🄳 DRINK

The Cocktail Geeks *(p79)*
The Devil's Advocate *(p73)*
Ecco Vino *(p75)*
Under the Stairs *(p77)*

🅂 SHOP

Armstrongs Vintage *(p88)*
I.J. Mellis *(p100)*
Little Blue Door Vintage *(p90)*
The Red Door Gallery *(p106)*
Underground Solu'shn *(p95)*
Walker Slater *(p107)*

🄰 ARTS &
CULTURE

Anatomical Museum *(p115)*
Bedlam Theatre *(p126)*
Brass Monkey *(p121)*
Dovecot Studios *(p128)*
Festival Theatre *(p125)*
Fruitmarket Gallery *(p117)*
Museum of Childhood *(p118)*

National Museum
    of Scotland *(p116)*
Scotsman Picturehouse *(p122)*
Stills *(p130)*
Surgeons' Hall Museums *(p118)*
The Writers' Museum *(p112)*

🄽 NIGHTLIFE

Bannerman's *(p143)*
The Banshee Labyrinth *(p145)*
The Bongo Club *(p149)*
Cabaret Voltaire *(p150)*
Captain's Bar *(p160)*
Department of Magic:
    Prophecies Quest *(p159)*
The Jazz Bar *(p141)*
La Belle Angele *(p150)*
The Liquid Room *(p140)*
The Mash House *(p149)*
Paradise Palms *(p152)*
The Royal Oak *(p163)*
Sandy Bell's *(p163)*
Sneaky Pete's *(p148)*
Stramash *(p140)*
Whistle Binkies *(p145)*
Wings *(p159)*

🄾 OUTDOORS

Royal Mile *(p173)*

MAP 2

BROUGHTON

2

D The Cumberland Bar

ABERCROMBY PLACE

Gardens

STREET

D Bramble
E Chez Jules

S Scottish Design Exchange

N El Barrio

STREET

D Hoot the Redeemer

THE MOUND

A Scottish National Gallery

OLD TOWN

ESPLANADE

JOHNSTON TERRACE

Cold Town House
D

GRASSMARKET

S **E** Mary's Milk Bar
Godiva Boutique

N The Wee Red Bar

LAURISTON PLACE

E EAT

Bell's Diner *(p43)*
Chez Jules *(p48)*
Grams *(p39)*
Greek Artisan Pastries *(p38)*
Kanpai *(p46)*
Lovecrumbs *(p53)*
Mary's Milk Bar *(p52)*
The Pantry *(p32)*
Timberyard *(p45)*
Vesta Bar & Kitchen *(p43)*

D DRINK

The Antiquary *(p66)*
Bon Vivant *(p75)*
Bramble *(p78)*
Cairngorm Coffee *(p61)*
The Cambridge Bar *(p65)*
The Chaumer *(p75)*
Cold Town House *(p69)*
The Cumberland Bar *(p68)*
The Hanging Bat *(p83)*
Hoot the Redeemer *(p77)*
The Last Word Saloon *(p79)*
The Lucky Liquor Co. *(p78)*
Panda & Sons *(p78)*
Smith & Gertrude *(p73)*
Tigerlily *(p76)*

S SHOP

ANTA Scotland *(p106)*
Armchair Books *(p99)*
Assai Records *(p92)*

Carnivàle Vintage *(p91)*
Godiva Boutique *(p88)*
Miss Bizio Couture *(p89)*
Scottish Design Exchange *(p105)*
Stockbridge Market *(p102)*
Those Were the Days *(p91)*
Vox Box *(p93)*

A ARTS & CULTURE

Edinburgh Castle *(p112)*
The Filmhouse *(p120)*
The Lyceum *(p124)*
Scottish National Gallery *(p118)*
Traverse Theatre *(p124)*
The Usher Hall *(p127)*

N NIGHTLIFE

4042 *(p156)*
The Black Cat *(p161)*
El Barrio *(p151)*
Fingers Piano Bar *(p144)*
Ghillie Dhu *(p160)*
Henry's Cellar Bar *(p142)*
Lulu *(p151)*
NQ64 Arcade Bar *(p158)*
Supercube *(p158)*
The Wee Red Bar *(p150)*

O OUTDOORS

Dean Village *(p174)*
Princes Street Gardens *(p168)*

0 metres 250
0 yards 250

Casa Amiga **E**

Elvis Shakespeare **S**
Epoca **S**

CANONMILLS

BROUGHTON ROAD

EAST CLAREMONT STREET

PILRIG STREET
DRYDEN STREET
LEITH

MCDONALD ROAD

ANNANDALE STREET

S The Marshmallow Lady
E The Bearded Baker

E Bodega Taqueria
E The Little Chartroom

BELLEVUE

LONDON STREET

DRUMMOND PLACE

BROUGHTON

Typewronger Books
McNaughton's **S**
Bookshop

LEITH WALK
BRUNSWICK
MONTGOMERY STREET

Pickles **D**
E
D The Barony
D Artisan
Roast

S Valvona & Crolla

S Vinyl Villains

Ingleby Gallery **A**
New Town Deli **A**

ALBANY STREET

Embassy Gallery **A** **D**
Fore Play Crazy Golf **N**
The Street **N** **N**
Uno Mas

The
Outhouse

Planet Bar
& Kitchen

N **S** Topping &
Company

N CC Blooms
N Café Habana

LONDON ROAD

E
The Gardener's
Cottage

Royal
Terrace Gardens

YORK PLACE

GREENSIDE

CALTON

Nightcap
A **N** **D** **A** The Stand Comedy Club
Fortitude

Scottish National
Portrait Gallery

Regent
Gardens

ST ANDREW SQUARE

Collective **A**
O
Calton
Hill

Melville Monument **A**

LEITH STREET

N The Bunker

E The Dome
D
Rose Street
Garden

Lady **N**
Libertine
N The Voodoo
Rooms

A Old Calton
Cemetery

REGENT ROAD

PRINCES STREET
WAVERLEY BRIDGE

STREET
NORTH BRIDGE

Edinburgh
Waverley
Station

CALTON ROAD

NEW STREET

The People's Story
Museum
A

CANONGATE
REIDS CLOSE

S Scottish
Poetry
Library

EAST MARKET STREET

OLD TOWN

HIGH STREET

CANONGATE

MAP 3

IONA STREET

LMENY ST

3

A Out of the Blue Drill Hall

ALBERT STREET

ROAD

EASTER

Little Fitzroy **D**
Polentoni **E**

The Regent **N**

REGENT ROAD

ABBEYMOUNT

ABBEYHILL

ABBEYHILL

HOLYROOD

Scottish Parliament

A Dynamic Earth

E EAT

The Bearded Baker *(p53)*
Bodega Taqueria *(p51)*
Casa Amiga *(p54)*
The Dome *(p44)*
The Gardener's Cottage *(p44)*
The Little Chartroom *(p46)*
New Town Deli *(p36)*
Polentoni *(p34)*

D DRINK

Artisan Roast *(p61)*
The Barony *(p64)*
Fortitude *(p60)*
Little Fitzroy *(p63)*
The Outhouse *(p71)*
Pickles *(p73)*
Rose Street Garden *(p71)*

S SHOP

Elvis Shakespeare *(p93)*
Epoca *(p90)*
The Marshmallow Lady *(p103)*
McNaughtan's Bookshop *(p98)*
Scottish Poetry Library *(p99)*
Topping & Company *(p96)*
Typewronger Books *(p96)*
Valvona & Crolla *(p102)*
Vinyl Villains *(p92)*

A ARTS & CULTURE

Collective *(p131)*
Dynamic Earth *(p117)*
Embassy Gallery *(p128)*
Ingleby Gallery *(p130)*
Melville Monument *(p113)*
Old Calton Cemetery *(p113)*
Out of the Blue Drill Hall *(p133)*
The People's Story Museum *(p114)*
Scottish National Portrait Gallery *(p119)*
The Stand Comedy Club *(p125)*

N NIGHTLIFE

The Bunker *(p144)*
Café Habana *(p154)*
CC Blooms *(p154)*
Fore Play Crazy Golf *(p158)*
Lady Libertine *(p147)*
Nightcap *(p147)*
Planet Bar & Kitchen *(p153)*
The Regent *(p153)*
The Street *(p152)*
The Voodoo Rooms *(p141)*
Uno Mass *(p147)*

O OUTDOORS

Calton Hill *(p174)*

The Wee Museum of Memory Ⓐ

Vue Ocean Terminal Ⓐ

OCEAN DRIVE

Victoria Dock

Albert Dock

LINDSAY ROAD

OCEAN DRIVE

Ⓞ The Shore

Teuchters Landing Ⓓ

Alby's Ⓔ

PORTLAND STREET

COMMERCIAL STREET

NORTH JUNCTION STREET

Custom Lane Ⓐ Ⓢ Kestin
Ⓓ Williams & Johnson

Port of Leith Distillery Ⓓ

Café Domenico Ⓔ

Ⓓ Carriers Quarters

BERNARD ST

Ostara Ⓔ

Coburg House Art Studios Ⓐ Ⓔ Roseleaf

Ⓔ Restaurant
Ⓔ Martin Wishart

Ⓓ Toast

Leith Theatre Ⓐ

SHORE

LEITH

FERRY ROAD

Water of Leith

Ⓐ Sketchy Beats Café

Crolla's Ⓔ Gelataria

TOLBOOTH WYND

CONSTITUTION STREET

The Pitt Ⓐ

The Tartan Blanket Co. Ⓐ

HENDERSON STREET

Ⓔ Borough Restaurant

ANDERSON PLACE

BANGOR ROAD

GREAT JUNCTION STREET

Ⓐ Trinity House Maritime Museum

The Biscuit Factory Ⓐ

Campervan Brewery Ⓓ

Razzo Ⓔ

Ⓢ Good Vibes

DUKE STREET

DUNCAN PLACE

Leith Links West

BONNINGTON ROAD

Logan Malloch Ltd Ⓢ

HERMITAG

Pilrig Park

LEITH WALK

Nauticus Ⓓ Ⓢ Twelve Triangles

LOCHEND ROAD

PILRIG STREET

Ⓔ Bross Bagels

Leith Depot Ⓝ

HALMYRE STREET

EASTER ROAD

BALFOUR STREET

Ⓔ Knights Kitchen

Mousetrap Ⓝ

Origano Ⓔ

Ⓓ Abode Bar

0 metres   250
0 yards   250

MAP 4

4

*Edinburgh
Dock*

Cutting Chaii 🖲

SALAMANDER STREET

SALAMANDER PLACE

LINKS PLACE

PLACE   East Coast 🆂
Cured

EAST RESTALRIG TERRACE

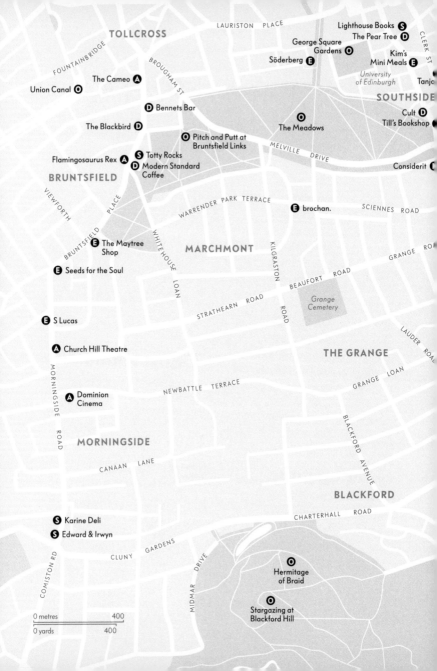

LAURISTON PLACE

TOLLCROSS

Lighthouse Books **S**
The Pear Tree **D**

George Square
Gardens **O**

Söderberg **E**

Kim's
Mini Meals **E**

FOUNTAINBRIDGE

BROUGHAM ST

The Cameo **A**

University
of Edinburgh

Tanje

SOUTHSIDE

Union Canal **O**

Cult **D**
Till's Bookshop **O**

D Bennets Bar

The Blackbird **D**

O Pitch and Putt at
Bruntsfield Links

The Meadows **O**

MELVILLE DRIVE

Considerit **O**

Flamingosaurus Rex **A**
S Totty Rocks
D Modern Standard
Coffee

E brochan.

SCIENNES ROAD

BRUNTSFIELD

VIEWFORTH

WARRENDER PARK TERRACE

MARCHMONT

GRANGE RO

BRUNTSFIELD PLACE

E The Maytree
Shop

WHITEHOUSE LOAN

KILGRASTON ROAD

BEAUFORT ROAD

E Seeds for the Soul

STRATHEARN ROAD

Grange
Cemetery

ROAD

E S Lucas

LAUDER ROAD

A Church Hill Theatre

THE GRANGE

MORNINGSIDE ROAD

NEWBATTLE TERRACE

GRANGE LOAN

A Dominion
Cinema

BLACKFORD AVENUE

MORNINGSIDE

CANAAN LANE

BLACKFORD

CHARTERHALL ROAD

S Karine Deli

S Edward & Irwyn

GARDENS

COMISTON RD

CLUNY GARDENS

MIDMAR DRIVE

O
Hermitage
of Braid

0 metres   400

0 yards   400

O
Stargazing at
Blackford Hill

Holyrood Park

ackbeat

Holyrood Distillery Ⓓ

The High Dive Ⓝ

5

The Queen's Hall

arney's eer

Ⓓ Pickering's Gin

Ⓓ Ⓐ Summerhall

he oyal Dick

NEWINGTON ROAD

MAYFIELD ROAD

WEST SAVILE TERRACE

WEST MAINS ROAD

MAP 5

Ⓔ EAT

brochan. *(p34)*

Considerit *(p55)*

Kim's Mini Meals *(p50)*

The Maytree Shop *(p54)*

Seeds for the Soul *(p40)*

S Lucas *(p55)*

Söderberg *(p35)*

Tanjore *(p49)*

Ⓓ DRINK

Barney's Beer *(p81)*

Bennets Bar *(p65)*

The Blackbird *(p70)*

Cult *(p63)*

Holyrood Distillery *(p83)*

Modern Standard Coffee *(p63)*

The Pear Tree *(p68)*

Pickering's Gin *(p82)*

The Royal Dick *(p70)*

Ⓢ SHOP

Backbeat *(p95)*

Edward & Irwyn *(p100)*

Karine Deli *(p101)*

Lighthouse Books *(p99)*

Till's Bookshop *(p98)*

Totty Rocks *(p106)*

Ⓐ ARTS & CULTURE

The Cameo *(p120)*

Church Hill Theatre *(p127)*

Dominion Cinema *(p120)*

Flamingosaurus Rex *(p131)*

Summerhall *(p132)*

Ⓝ NIGHTLIFE

The High Dive *(p145)*

The Queen's Hall *(p143)*

Ⓞ OUTDOORS

George Square Gardens *(p171)*

Hermitage of Braid *(p172)*

The Meadows *(p168)*

Pitch and Putt at Bruntsfield Links *(p183)*

Stargazing at Blackford Hill *(p183)*

Union Canal *(p172)*

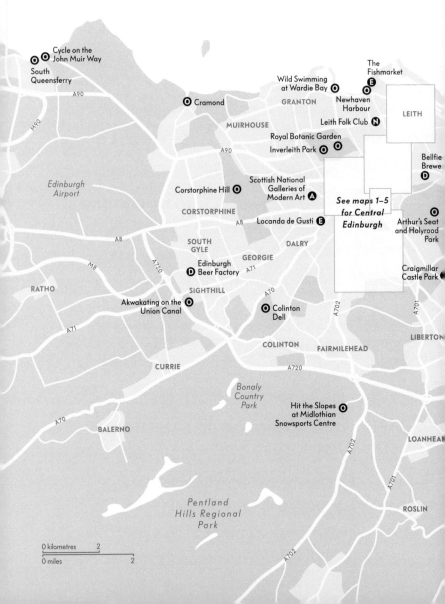

Firth of Forth

Cycle on the
John Muir Way

South
Queensferry

The
Fishmarket

Wild Swimming
at Wardie Bay

Cramond

GRANTON

Newhaven
Harbour

LEITH

MUIRHOUSE

Leith Folk Club

A90

Royal Botanic Garden

Inverleith Park

Bellfie
Brewe

Edinburgh
Airport

Corstorphine Hill

Scottish National
Galleries of
Modern Art

CORSTORPHINE

See maps 1–5
for Central
Edinburgh

A8

Locanda de Gusti

Arthur's Seat
and Holyrood
Park

A8

DALRY

SOUTH
GYLE

GEORGIE

Craigmillar
Castle Park

A720

Edinburgh
Beer Factory

M8

A71

RATHO

SIGHTHILL

A70

A702

A701

Akwakating on the
Union Canal

Colinton
Dell

LIBERTON

A71

COLINTON

FAIRMILEHEAD

CURRIE

A720

Bonaly
Country
Park

Hit the Slopes
at Midlothian
Snowsports Centre

A70

BALERNO

LOANHEA

A702

A701

Pentland
Hills Regional
Park

ROSLIN

A702

0 kilometres   2

0 miles   2

MAP 6

6

🇪 EAT

The Fishmarket *(p40)*
Locanda de Gusti *(p48)*

🇩 DRINK

Bellfield Brewery *(p82)*
Edinburgh Beer Factory *(p82)*

🇸 SHOP

Portobello Bookshop *(p97)*

🇦 ARTS & CULTURE

Scottish National Galleries
of Modern Art *(p119)*
St Margaret's House *(p135)*

🇳 NIGHTLIFE

Leith Folk Club *(p163)*
The Sheep Heid Inn *(p157)*

🇴 OUTDOORS

Akwakating on the
Union Canal *(p180)*
Arthur's Seat and
Holyrood Park *(p170)*
Colinton Dell *(p175)*
Corstorphine Hill *(p175)*
Craigmillar Castle Park *(p171)*
Cramond *(p178)*
Cycle on the John
Muir Way *(p181)*
Dr Neil's Garden *(p170)*
East Lothian Coast *(p179)*
Hit the Slopes at Midlothian
Snowsports Centre *(p181)*
Inverleith Park *(p169)*
Newhaven Harbour *(p177)*
Portobello *(p176)*
Royal Botanic Garden *(p169)*
South Queensferry *(p178)*
Wild Swimming at
Wardie Bay *(p180)*

A199

Portobello
Bookshop Portobello
🇸 🇴

Margaret's
ouse

The Sheep Heid Inn
Dr Neil's Garden

CRAIGMILLAR

🇴
East Lothian Coast
40 km (25 miles)

A7

A772

GILMERTON

A720

A768

BONNYRIGG

A6094

OSEWELL

EAT

Michelin-starred fine dining that champions local flavours or a heart-warming pub tea with pals: eating out in Edinburgh doesn't have to be fancy, but it's always fun.

Breakfast and Brunch

The most important meal of the day. Whether you fancy a pastry to go or a full Scottish (haggis, tattie scones and all), this city has you covered.

OSTARA

Map 4; 52 Coburg Street, Leith; ///oval.edgy.elbow; www.ostaracafe.co.uk

Hidden away on a quiet cobbled street by the Water of Leith, this neighbourhood bistro is loved by locals in the know. And what do they order? The kimchi chilli scrambled eggs followed by winter-spiced French toast for a perfect breakfast pud. What better start to the day?

THE PANTRY

Map 2; 1 North West Circus Place, Stockbridge; ///sketch.coffee.bets; www.thepantryedinburgh.co.uk

Brunch at the Pantry is a classy affair – no surprise given its genteel Stockbridge surroundings and well-heeled clientele. But for all its airs and graces, this place is famed for its Pantry Fry, a feast of a fry-up featuring rare-breed pork sausages and Stornoway black pudding. Not big on meat? One half of the food-loving duo running the joint

Here on a Sunday? Head to Stockbridge Market *(p102)* for culinary treats and creative local crafts.

is a staunch veggie so the Pantry serves up some stellar meat alternatives like sweet potato rosti with poached eggs, grilled courgettes, smoked paprika and halloumi.

EDINBURGH LARDER

Map 1; 15 Blackfriars Street, Old Town; ///pines.verge.nurse; www.edinburghlarder.co.uk

Away from the usual tourist spots on the Royal Mile is this wee gem. You'll be greeted with a warm welcome and the oh-so-comforting aroma of freshly ground coffee, plus the finest locally sourced produce prepared with love and care. The friendly chatter of full and contented diners fills this cosy space – a sure sign you're in the right spot. So grab a table and enjoy perfectly poached eggs Florentine and a cup of top-quality, locally roasted coffee.

» Don't leave without popping next door to the adorable Little Larder for takeaway brunch options and some gorgeous giftable goodies like Scottish heather honey, handmade soap, candles and pottery.

Try it!
CREATIVE MORNINGS

Looking for some creative stimulation to start your day? Creative Mornings runs free monthly breakfast events featuring a guest speaker, plenty of scran and coffee galore *(www.creativemornings.com/cities/edi)*.

POLENTONI

Map 3; 38 Easter Road, Abbeyhill; ///plot.soft.chats; 0131 661 6182

Get yourself over to Polentoni ASAP for hearty brunch dishes, great coffee-to-go and a deli counter bursting at the seams with mouth-watering Italian goodies. And you can sit in too – this cosy café is always packed with hungry Easter Road locals keen to try whatever daily special chef Franco is cooking up in his tiny kitchen.

BROCHAN.

Map 5; 24 Marchmont Crescent, Marchmont; ///spin.tell.sides; www.brochan.co.uk

In the eyes of Scots porridge purists, adding anything other than water to your morning gruel is totally out of the question. But at brochan., all rules are out the window. Tuck into a scrumptious breakfast bowl of hand-rolled Scottish oats piled high with rainbow toppings like blueberry compote, bee pollen, pomegranate, popcorn (yup, you read it right) or ginger poached pear. Complete your gourmet breakfast experience with a Hawaiian smoothie, matcha latte or freshly squeezed orange juice and you're on to a right winner.

ROSELEAF

Map 4; 23–24 Sandport Place, Leith; ///much.poem.float; www.roseleaf.co.uk

There's just something about the Roseleaf. Maybe it's the zany décor and array of curious hats suspended from the ceiling. Maybe it's the chunky wooden bar that dates back to 1900. Or perhaps it's the fact that the menus are hidden inside vintage Nat Geo mags and prices are listed exclusively in pennies. The food's pretty special too. Choose from a range of creative yet comforting classics like shakshuka, fancy fungi on toast or, or if you're really hungry, "the big yin", and enjoy. Oh, and breakfast cocktails are served in teapots, naturally.

SÖDERBERG
Map 5; 27 Simpson Loan, Quartermile; ///wink.blend.entertainer;
www.soderberg.uk

This Scandi-chic bakery is where you'll find Edinburgh Uni students catching up over cardamom buns or ploughing through reading lists while enjoying a much-needed caffeine fix. On rare sunny days sit outside and watch bespectacled professors dash to their next lecture, avoiding wannabe skateboarders practising their kickflips.

CITY CAFÉ
Map 1; 19 Blair Street, Old Town; ///decreased.prop.select;
www.thecitycafe.co.uk

Breakfast at the City Café is fun. Open early till late, this classic "caff" can be whatever you need it to be: hangover brekkie haven; an afternoon spot for pints and pool; or a busy bar with great DJs and cocktails. But back to breakfast. Plates are filled with a full Scottish or stacks of fluffy American-style pancakes. Expect lashings of maple syrup, massive milkshakes and a steaming cup of joe.

» Don't leave without having a go on the awesome vintage jukebox – but be prepared to have your tunes scrutinized by your fellow diners.

Lunch Spots

Cute wee cafés, legendary takeaway joints and rave-reviewed restaurants offering lunchtime bargains: Edinburgh has more than its fair share of lunchtime pit stops to keep local tums full throughout the day.

TUPINIQUIM

Map 1; Green Police Box, Lauriston Place, Southside; ///cooper.factor.forget; www.tupiniquim.co.uk

This Tardis-like home kitchen is a culinary carnival in a converted police box. It may be tiny, but the flavours (and personalities) here are anything but. Serving up their delicious gluten-free Brazilian crepes to hungry Southsiders since they first opened in 2010, owners Fernando and Gardenia can't help but spoil you by jazzing up your order with an extra sprinkle of this and that.

NEW TOWN DELI

Map 3; 23 Henderson Row, Stockbridge; ///wounds.modest.begin; www.thenewtowndeli.com

Homemade soup, a colourful salad box or a tasty toasted flatbread with your choice of filling: lunch comes in many forms at the beloved New Town Deli. Championing fresh ingredients from local suppliers, this stylish spot is great for a light, healthy lunch packed full of flavour. Make like the locals and combine this with a made-to-order berry blast smoothie to get you that bit closer to your five-a-day goal.

CAFÉ DOMENICO

Map 4; 30 Sandport Street, Leith; ///charmingly.prop.stands; www.cafedomenico.co.uk

Famed for its bizarre yet brilliant toasted wraps, Café Domenico tempts Leith creatives away from their industrial-chic offices and straight through its doors with such creative concoctions as nduja, nachos and macaroni cheese – yup, all in one wrap. If the wraps don't take your fancy, nab a table for an easy-eating plate of pasta and other Italian classics at an insanely affordable price.

THE OUTSIDER

Map 1; 15 George IV Bridge, Old Town; ///button.bridge.design; www.outsiderrestaurant.co.uk

This upmarket restaurant is always fully booked for dinner, but savvy locals know to come here for the budget-friendly lunch menu instead. Steamed Scottish mussels with smoked bacon in a buttery white wine sauce served with garlicky fries, all for under eight quid? Unbeatable. Order the artisan bread and olives while you wait and feel smug in the knowledge that you've bagged yourself a bargain, and a delicious one at that.

» Don't leave without taking a peek out of the huge windows at the back of the restaurant for an incredible castle view.

GREEK ARTISAN PASTRIES

Map 2; 23 Bread Street, Tollcross;

///doors.chains.scope; www.artisonfoodsltd.co.uk

Get your hands on a feast of flaky filo parcels crammed full with moreish Greek-inspired fillings at this oh-so-wonderful pastry shop. The vibe is mega casual and the service is the friendliest in town. Trust us when we say you won't be able to resist a slice of the walnut and honey syrup cake afterwards.

ALBY'S

Map 4; 8 Portland Place, Leith;

///judges.zealous.fakes; www.albysleith.co.uk

Big, piping hot sandwiches are Alby's mainstay, and boy, they are magnificent. Owned by Matt, Tash and their dog Alby, this place has become one of Leith's coolest lunch spots. Expect killer combos,

Shh!

You may have heard of the Elephant House Café of wizarding fame. These days it's more of a tourist draw than a local haunt. Just a stone's throw away, Elephants and Bagels *(37 Marshall Street)* is the lesser-known sister café, popular among students and budding writers seeking their own stroke of inspiration. Complete with a gallery of customers' crayon drawings (of elephants of course), we're pretty sure the magical creative vibes have relocated – keep the secret.

all served on generously sliced focaccia. And truly anything goes here. Vegan? Options like turmeric roasted cauliflower with sumac onions and pomegranate are often the star of the day. After something a bit different? Try salt and chilli squid, steak bavette, pak choi and pickled chillies with Tom Yum mayo and a side of paneer fries.

» **Don't leave without** picking up some of Alby's signature sandwich merch – it's become a staple in a fair few local wardrobes.

GRAMS

Map 2; 68 Hamilton Place, Stockbridge;
///link.toxic.again; www.gramsedinburgh.com

Grams is dedicated to crafting quick, scrumptious, and good-for-you meals in an uber-stylish pink-and-white tiled setting. Grab a table and tuck right in to some gluten-free pulled-pork nachos or vegan banana waffles and you'll witness a steady rotation of well-dressed socialites snapping a quick selfie before tucking in to a burrito box.

BROSS BAGELS

Map 4; 6 Manderston Street, Leith; ///elite.quarrel.game;
www.brossbagels.com

Edinburgh has gone bagel mad, and it's entirely down to Montreal native Larah Bross. Her New York deli-style bagel stores are rarely without queues out the door. First, select your bagel: poppy seed, pretzel or chipotle (to name just a few). Then, your filling: pastrami, Montreal slaw, melted jack cheese, fried pickles, kimchi sauce, jalapenos, smoked *facon* – the combinations are endless.

Comfort Food

*The perfect antidote to Edinburgh's long, cold
winters, comfort food is all about bringing gangs of
hungry mates together over hearty and warming
dishes that deliver all the feels.*

THE FISHMARKET

**Map 6; 23A Pier Place, Newhaven; ///email.point.swim;
www.thefishmarketnewhaven.co.uk**

Fish 'n' chips are comfort food 101, and the much-loved classic
has been taken up a notch at this top-class chippy. Sit in and join
the animated chatter in the busy seafood restaurant, or take away
to enjoy your fish supper by the water's edge, soundtracked by gulls
flying overhead. Be careful though: a plucky few have been known
to swoop down on unsuspecting diners in pursuit of a chip (or three).

SEEDS FOR THE SOUL

**Map 5; 167 Bruntsfield Place, Bruntsfield; ///engage.cages.love;
www.seedsforthesoul.co.uk**

Twinkling fairy lights adorn this ferociously ethical vegan café, where
fists (and paws) for liberation are stamped on the menu. Join an
eco-conscious crowd as they chow down on guilt-free burgers or opt

for the ultimate comforting Canadian import, vegan poutine (yup, chips, dairy-free cheese curds and gravy). Or maybe your idea of comfort is a green smoothie and a heathy salad bowl? If so, you're in the right place: comfort comes in many forms, and it doesn't need to be deep-fried to give you that warm, fuzzy feeling.

RAZZO

Map 4; 59 Great Junction Street, Leith; ///glaze.bond.plan; www.razzopizza.co.uk

From their shoebox pizzeria, new(ish) kids on the block Razzo have taken Leith by storm. Tuck into authentic Neapolitan pizzas topped with roasted aubergine, artichoke or spicy salami. Value for money is through the roof here, and you'll struggle to find few things as life-affirming as the soft Razzo dough. Leith locals have been known to liken the crusts to pillows made of clouds.

» **Don't leave without** trying the *burrata e capocollo* – there's a whole burrata in the middle of the pizza. We repeat, a whole burrata.

ARCADE HAGGIS AND WHISKY HOUSE

Map 1; 48 Cockburn Street, Old Town; ///dare.shed.plus; www.arcadepub.co.uk

Okay, we can't not mention haggis. Usually served with neeps and tatties (turnip and mashed potatoes, for those not in the know), this peppery pudding is the ultimate in hearty dining. You'll spot haggis on many a Scottish menu, but Arcades gives it a fun twist by serving it on cheesy nachos or as scrummy fried bon bons. Need we say more?

Solo, Pair, Crowd

Whether it's a table for one or supper with the whole squad, this city has some stellar options for hearty scran.

FLYING SOLO
Soup for the soul
There are few things as comforting as a hearty bowl of soup. Head to dedicated soup café Union of Genius, grab a window seat and cradle a comforting bowl of hot broth as you watch the world go by.

IN A PAIR
Tapas for two
Date night? Make a beeline for Leith's Tapa for a cosy candlelit dining experience. In this gorgeously romantic setting, feast yourself on too many tapas and enjoy Spanish comfort food at its best.

FOR A CROWD
Pizza with pals
Trendy New York-style pizza parlour Civerinos is perfect for a big group of pals. With communal tables and jaw-dropping 20-inch pizzas, there'll be a slice for everyone. Nothing brightens a rainy day like never-ending pepperoni pizza.

MOSQUE KITCHEN

Map 1; 31 Nicolson Square, Southside;
///monday.crash.woof; www.mosquekitchen.com

At the Mosque Kitchen comfort comes in paper bowls full of steaming daal and chicken biryani. Run by the nearby mosque, this canteen-style curry house has been filling the hungry tums of savvy Southsiders and penny-pinching students for decades.

BELL'S DINER

Map 2; 7 St Stephen Street, Stockbridge;
///nature.refers.straw; www.bellsdineredinburgh.co.uk

Locals have been going to Bell's since they were bairns. And after decades of pleasing punters with its homemade burgers, fries and shakes, this place has got casual dining pretty down. Not stuck in the past entirely, it has some great veggie and vegan options too.

VESTA BAR & KITCHEN

Map 2; 7–8 Queensferry Street, West End;
///alone.player.salsa; www.vestaedinburgh.co.uk

Vesta centres itself around the concept of home – and not just as an aesthetic goal. Partnered with the Social Bite movement, the team behind Vesta are on a mission to end homelessness in the city one meal at a time. As for the menu, you'll find pub grub classics with a gourmet surprise. Tuck into this nourishing take on social justice.

» Don't leave without paying forward the cost of a coffee or meal for people experiencing homelessness.

Special Occasion

Swap deep-fried Mars bars for Michelin stars – you're celebrating after all. Edinburgh is the perfect place to sample Scotland's culinary prowess and enjoy a memorable meal in some pretty magical settings.

THE DOME

Map 3; 14 George Street, New Town;
///format.skips.zeal; www.thedomeedinburgh.com

When the locals are feeling fancy and want to flaunt it, the Dome is where they go. Sitting pretty on one of the city's swankiest streets, the palatial facade is impressive enough, but inside is a whole other ball game. Think floral sprays, pillared arches, obscene amounts of marble and a glass-domed ceiling. As well as serving a modern Scottish menu, it's also a great spot for cocktails and afternoon tea.

THE GARDENER'S COTTAGE

Map 3; 1 London Road, Abbeyhill;
///bids.dunes.slim; www.thegardenerscottage.co.uk

Once upon a time this cosy cottage was the Royal Gardener's home; today it's the city's most homely spot for posh nosh. Try the seven-course tasting menu, starring seasonal British ingredients grown in the back garden and lovingly prepared in the tiny open kitchen. Don't be shy, cosy up at communal tables and share the experience with your fellow diners – you'll be best pals by the end of the night.

» Don't leave without opting in on the paired wines. A different drink comes with every dish, perfectly matched to each course.

TIMBERYARD

Map 2; 10 Lady Lawson Street, Old Town;
///sheep.head.dance; www.timberyard.co

Timberyard's signature big red door is a portal into an industrial-chic wonderland. Here, bearded servers with tattoo sleeves shower you with stunning Scottish cuisine artfully presented on equally stunning stoneware. So go on, celebrate with a slap-up meal, and toast that well-deserved promotion with a weird yet wonderfully earthy cocktail garnished with... is that moss?

ORIGANO

Map 4; 236 Leith Walk, Leith;
///clocks.models.wage; www.origano-leith.co.uk

If perfect pizza is an integral part of a perfect evening (as it should be), then Origano is for you. A great place for a romantic evening, Origano promises a sea of candlelight, intimate tables and a warm, buzzy atmosphere. From the open kitchen, the aroma of wood-fired pizza fills the room. This place is a welcome reminder that special doesn't necessarily mean spenny: antipasti boards are generous, the service is top-notch and the setting is, simply put, bangin'.

KANPAI

Map 2; 8 Grindlay Street, Tollcross; ///active.script.parks;
www.kanpaisushiedinburgh.co.uk

The name Kanpai translates as cheers and, since this standout
Japanese joint serves up some of the finest sushi in the city, a toast
is most definitely in order. The menu here includes some authentic
(read: unusual) selections alongside the big-hitters you'd expect.
» Don't leave without trying the miso aubergine. Or why not
splash out on the snow crab special? You're celebrating after all.

BOROUGH RESTAURANT

Map 4; 50 Henderson Street, Leith;
///porch.taking.ridge; www.boroughrestaurant.com

Proving that special can also be simple, dinner at this neighbourhood
eatery promises a spectacular meal without the fuss (or hefty price
tag). Brainchild of husband and wife duo Darren and Aleks, Borough
is the perfect place for that celebratory birthday tea — treat yourself
to the four-course set menu featuring scrummy Scottish classics or
pass perfectly executed small plates around your loved ones.

THE LITTLE CHARTROOM

Map 3; 30 Albert Place, Leith;
///latest.dogs.loving; www.thelittlechartroom.com

Head chef and Edinburgh lass Roberta Hall-McCarron has become
something of a celebrity in Scotland's culinary world, and this tiny,
almost fine-dining joint, set up by Roberta and her husband Sean,

shows why. Contemporary Scottish cuisine reaches whole new heights here, with big flavours dominating a minimalist menu. Think torched mackerel with barbequed peach, or monkfish with bacon and clams. Perch at the bar and watch The Little Chartroom turn cooking into art.

RESTAURANT MARTIN WISHART

Map 4; 54 Shore, Leith;
///pounds.king.agenda; www.restaurantmartinwishart.co.uk

Graduation dinners, engagement celebrations: life's big moments are marked by Edinburgers and their nearest and dearest here. Even if you're not familiar with its namesake restaurateur and head-chef, this Michelin-starred dining experience will dazzle you with top-of-the-range tasting menus in a luxury setting. While local ingredients are standard in these parts, Wishart's creative flair and finely tuned French cooking technique really make them sing. Parents in town? Perfect, just make sure they're footing the bill.

When the moon is full, head to the outskirts of the city for an enchanting dining experience at the Secret Herb Garden (www.secretherbgarden.co.uk). A short stroll past the fairy wood and gin garden will bring you to a long, supper club-style table in a spacious glasshouse. Here you'll enjoy a four-course meal prepared by rotating guest chefs. Break bread beneath the stars, among botanicals, flowers and, of course, good company.

Scran of the World

Edinburgh is becoming more multicultural by the minute, and nowhere is this more evident than in the sheer variety of cuisines available. This city's foodie scene is well and truly a global affair.

CHEZ JULES

Map 2; 109 Hanover Street, New Town;
///ripe.motion.engage; www.chezjulesbistro.com

Welcome to this adorable wee slice of old-school France, where red-and-white gingham tablecloths are topped with wax-coated wine bottles that double as candleholders. Locals rave about the lunchtime *prix fixe* menu here, which offers hearty French classics like French onion soup and skirt steak with pommes frites, paired with a jovial glass of Côtes du Rhône, *bien sûr*.

LOCANDA DE GUSTI

Map 6; 102 Dalry Road, Dalry;
///organs.rats.much; www.locandadegusti.com

This family-run Italian trattoria brings authentic (and need we say delicious?) Neapolitan cuisine to loyal Dalry denizens who keep the place deservedly busy. Seafood is the star of the show here; try Chef

Don't rush your meal – towards the end of the night you may get a *limoncello* on the house if you're lucky.

Rosario's lobster linguine, or go all in for the seafood platter – fresh Scottish seafood prepared with his Italian know-how is a match made in heaven. *Perfetto*!

TANJORE

Map 5; 6 Clerk Street, Newington;
///modes.shell.loses; www.tanjore.co.uk

Mrs Boon and her family keep the city's Southside fed with the best South Indian food in Edinburgh. This place epitomizes all that is wonderful about family-run, local businesses. Expect warm service, loyal regulars, and lovingly prepared food featuring truly authentic South Indian dishes that you may not have tried before. Oh, and being South Indian, it's a great spot for veggies. Add to that the fact that it's BYO and you'll begin to see why this place is loved by locals.

CUTTING CHAII

Map 4; 18 Salamander Street, Leith;
///cubs.moves.bikes; www.cuttingchaii.co.uk

Inspired by the old Iranian cafés of Mumbai, this fantastic curry house serves Indian food tapas style. Join hungry Leithers as they mix and match their thali platters and chow down on spicy chilli prawns and Bombay *benjan*. Inevitably they'll order way too much and waddle home in a contented food coma. But that's the whole point, right?

» Don't leave without trying Maa's butter chicken. Spicy, creamy and delicious, this is something of a signature dish at Cutting Chaii.

KIM'S MINI MEALS

Map 5; 5 Buccleuch Street, Newington; ///wipe.teeth.plot;
www.kimsminimeals.com

You'll definitely have to wait for a table at this family-run Korean joint. But it's worth it. Mr Kim's hospitality will make you grin, and once you're seated, Mama Kim will cook you up a kimchi storm in her tiny kitchen (if you're wondering what to order, the pork *bulgogi* is a must). The restaurant's slogan is "elegant and comfy, just like home" – we couldn't have put it better ourselves.

TING THAI CARAVAN

Map 1; 55 Lothian Road, Old Town;
///quarrel.universally.credit; www.tingthai-caravan.com

With its street food feel and slightly chaotic, high-energy vibe, this student hotspot has become a bit of a foodie fave for locals in the know. Ting's is all about authentic Thai cuisine that's not afraid to pack a punch. Try the creamy duck massaman for the ultimate indulgence or the Thai spicy beef salad for zingy chilli yumminess.
» Don't leave without washing down your pad thai with a Barney's Volcano IPA – it's the perfect accompaniment to Ting's zingy flavours.

KNIGHTS KITCHEN

Map 4; 166 Leith Walk; Leith; ///groom.snap.amber; 0131 667 7278

Owner and head chef Christine Knight (also known as Mama Knight) first introduced Edinburgers to scrumptious Kenyan soul food from her hugely popular stalls at the Leith and Stockbridge weekend markets. Now you can get your hands on Christine's life-affirming chicken and coconut curries, barbeque *boerewors* sausage rolls and moreish masala chips from her very own Leith shop, all served up with a generous helping of her trademark charm, of course. If the sun is shining, make hay and get your order to go – Leith Links is just up the road and the perfect spot for an alfresco bite.

BODEGA TAQUERIA

Map 3; 14 Albert Place, Leith;
///broad.stops.exam; www.ilovebodega.com

Channelling flavours from around the world in its signature soft-shell tacos, Bodega goes well beyond the remits of your typical Mexican taqueria. In fact, with fillings like buffalo cauliflower, spicy jerk chicken, Vietnamese pork and tempura tiger prawn, as well as the usual favourites (*carne assada*, tacos *al pastor* and Baja cod bites), we'd go so far as to say that this place is gloriously global. What's more, the sheer variety of cuisines on offer here make it the perfect choice for those who can never agree on what they fancy.

Try it!
COOK UP A STORM

Want to expand your culinary know-how? Edinburgh New Town Cookery School *(www.entcs.co.uk)* offers half- and full-day cooking classes specializing in cuisines from around the world.

Something Sweet

*The Scots have an insatiable sweet tooth, so it's no
surprise that Edinburgh is home to a plethora of
bakeries, ice cream parlours and sugar-fuelled shops
tempting locals with drool-worthy treats.*

MARY'S MILK BAR

Map 2; 19 Grassmarket, Old Town;
///soccer.solar.thin; www.marysmilkbar.com

Yorkshire-born Mary trained at a gelato university in Italy and, since
graduating (with flying colours we presume), her Milk Bar has
become a much-loved Edinburgh institution. The flavours here will
dazzle: choose from a changing daily selection such as white
chocolate peppermint, clementine sorbet, fried banana or even tea

Tucked away off Leith Walk is
the Sicilian Pastry Shop *(0131
554 7417)*. Head here for sweet
Sicilian pastries and enormous
cakes with lashings of whipped
cream, all at unbelievable prices.
Be sure to grab a cannoli to go;
they're stupidly good.

and jam. Or why not mix it up and go for a milkshake, hot chocolate or ice cream sundae? Whatever you choose, take your haul for a scenic wander around the Grassmarket's cobbled streets as you eat.

THE BEARDED BAKER

Map 3; 46 Rodney Street, Canonmills; ///hiding.jungle.clues; www.thebeardedbaker.co.uk

When Rowan (aka the Bearded Baker) posted his famous vegan cinnamon bun recipe online for amateur bakers to try at home, it was the talk of the town. That's the Bearded Baker all over – he just wants to share his sweet makes with the world. His shop presents a very select menu: perfect bakes only. Oh, and great coffee, of course. Pop in for an expertly brewed espresso and a satisfyingly sticky sugar-glazed doughnut.

LOVECRUMBS

Map 2; 155 West Port, Old Town; ///crust.cracks.goals; www.lovecrumbs.co.uk

Known for its towering displays of multi-tiered sponge cakes, Lovecrumbs simply radiates joy. Literally – a neon pink sign promises "nice times" and nice times you shall have. Adorably mismatched furnishings, granny-chic decor and succulents housed in teacups, this is where besties come for a good old sugary pick-me-up. Nab a spot by the piano or cosy up in a window box with your sweet treats.

>> Don't leave without checking out the wardrobe of cute stationery, loose leaf tea and coffee supplies to bring the good vibes home.

CROLLA'S GELATARIA

Map 4; 1 Coal Hill, Leith; ///shed.funded.clap; crollasgelateria.com

Irresistible puds piled high with fresh fruit and drizzled with chocolate sauce, stacks of fluffy Belgian waffles and ice cream sundaes straight from a Willy Wonka dreamland: for any sweet-toothed grown-up looking for their next dessert fix, Crolla's is the place to be. This Italian family-run ice cream parlour has been making traditional gelato in Scotland for over a century. And everything here is bigger, brighter and more sugary than is really acceptable, which is exactly what makes this place so wonderful.

THE MAYTREE SHOP

Map 5; 123 Bruntsfield Place, Bruntsfield; ///charge.wisdom.ocean; www.maytreeshop.co.uk

This neighbourhood *chocolaterie* invites sugar-seeking Bruntsfield residents to indulge in velvety-smooth artisan hot chocolate and a generous helping of homemade chocolate cake – and indulge they do. After something a bit lighter? Try the chocolate tea.

» Don't leave without perusing the wall of organic Fairtrade chocolate bars to take away as a gift (for yourself most likely, let's be honest).

CASA AMIGA

Map 3; 294 Leith Walk, Leith; ///tricky.drips.cars; www.casaamiga.co.uk

Casa Amiga translates as friendly house in Portuguese, and what's more welcoming than *pastéis de nata* by the half dozen? Their flaky pastry and warm, creamy centres tempt sweet-toothed locals from

Look around the groceries section of Casa Amiga and discover some great Portuguese products.

all over town down to Leith and through the doors of this Portuguese bakery. Word of warning: sticky fingers and a sugar rush are pretty much guaranteed.

S LUCAS

Map 5; 16 Morningside Road, Morningside;
///gift.third.salt; www.s-lucas.co.uk

Something of a sugary national treasure, the Lucas family have been making and selling their wonderful Italian dairy ice cream in Scotland for over a hundred years. Every day, fresh supplies are delivered from their signature shop and ice cream factory in nearby Musselburgh to their Morningside parlour. Here, young families and sugar addicts indulge in top-quality ice cream and a big scoop of Edinburgh history. For those with a particular love of all things sweet, the toffee fudgy wudgy is the cone for you.

CONSIDERIT

Map 5; 3–5A Sciennes, Newington;
///clay.vine.rocket; www.consideritchocolate.com

We all scream for plant-based ice cream. And doughnuts. And doughnuts filled with ice cream and drizzled with all the sauces and toppings of your vegan-friendly dreams. Vegans with a sweet tooth, listen up: this place has honey-free honeycomb and heaps of dairy-free ice cream flavours to choose from, depending on what's sold already. Get a boost on and get down here if you don't want to miss out.

A foodie day out from
city to sea

With an array of city-centre cafés and restaurants, it's easy to overlook those a little further afield. But that would be a mistake. Connecting the city to the Port of Leith is Leith Walk (dubbed "Eat Walk" by locals for its high concentration of foodie faves). Chaotic, a bit crumbly, but oh-so-charismatic, Leith is known for its strong sense of community. Shaped by waves of immigration, regeneration and, more recently, gentrification, the area wears its history (and heart) on its sleeve. And boy does it serve up some delicious global flavours.

1. Kilimanjaro Coffee
104 Nicolson Street, Old Town; 0131 662 0135
///report.puzzle.lock

2. Room and Rumours
25 East Market Street, Waverley Arches, Old Town
///limit.voice.much

3. Valvona & Crolla
19 Elm Row, Leith Walk
www.valvonacrolla.co.uk
///showed.images.rings

4. Punjabi Junction
122–4 Leith Walk, Leith;
www.punjabijunction.org
///amused.cloth.buzz

5. The Ship on the Shore
24–6 The Shore, Leith;
www.theshipontheshore.co.uk
///actors.influencing.tooth

Leith Farmers' Market
///goods.pads.combining

Leith Walk Police Box
///knots.tape.awake

GRANTON ROAD

FERRY ROAD

Royal Botan
Garden
Edinburgh

STOCKBRIDGE

WEST END

MORRISON STREE

HAYMARKET

NEWHAVEN

LINDSAY ROAD

NEWHAVEN ROAD

TRINITY

LEITH

SHORE

5

Splash out on dinner at THE SHIP ON THE SHORE

End your foodie day with some of Edinburgh's finest, fresh-as-it-gets seafood at this cosy shellfish and champagne spot, down by the waterfront.

Leith Farmers' Market
is held here every Saturday from 10am till 4pm; it's an absolute must for Edinburgh foodies.

CONSTITUTION ST

BROUGHTON RD

BROUGHTON

Water of Leith

4

Lunch at PUNJABI JUNCTION

This community-run social enterprise empowers minority ethnic women with training and employment opportunities. Pop in to pick up a jar of secret spice mix and you'll quickly realize you have to stay for lunch.

LEITH WALK

Leith Walk Police Box
is a much-loved pop-up space that owner Monty rents out to start-up kitchens, charities and budding creatives.

LOCHEND

LEITH WALK

3

Stock up at VALVONA & CROLLA

Putting prosciutto and parmesan on locals' plates since 1934, V&C is a pillar of Edinburgh's Scottish Italian community. Pick up some authentic Italian produce from the deli counter. *Bellissima.*

NEW TOWN

QUEEN STREET

PRINCES STREET

2

Satisfy your sweet tooth at ROOM AND RUMOURS

Rush to this friendly Edinburgh newbie to grab a freshly baked donut before they sell out. The flavours are eclectic and ever-changing, and the specialist coffees are sublime.

OLD TOWN

SOUTH BRIDGE

Edinburgh Castle

Holyrood Park

Breakfast at KILIMANJARO COFFEE

1

Start the day as you mean to go on with a hearty veggie or vegan breakfast at this heavenly city-centre brunch spot.

SOUTHSIDE

0 metres   750
0 yards   750

DRINK

Classic boozers, indie coffee shops and swanky cocktail joints are the heart of Edinburgh's social scene. Nothing beats catching up over a latte, or bantering beer in hand.

Coffee Shops

Edinburgh's bean scene is thriving, with independent cafés and secret coffee dens dotted all over the city. So whether yours is a macchiato or an oat milk latte, you're never too far from your next caffeine fix.

FORTITUDE

Map 3; 3C York Place, New Town; ///energy.decide.camps; www.fortitudecoffee.com

Sure, the coffee is great at Fortitude, but the people-watching? Even better. This tiny spot swarms with hipster professionals who come to browse an extensive menu of experimental roasts. Every time you see a napping French bulldog, a well-preened beard or someone engrossed in a chunky novel, down a shot (of natural Ethiopian espresso with floral notes, of course).

WILLIAMS & JOHNSON

Map 4; 1 Customs Wharf, Leith; ///eagles.trials.palms; www.williamsandjohnson.com

You may spot Williams & Johnson's postcard-sized roast cards in cafés across town, but this is where the magic happens. Pull up a chair at a clean and spacious communal table and sample single-

Sip your coffee while browsing the Lane's gallery space handily found in the same open-plan room.

origin seasonal espressos as you pretend not to eavesdrop on artists having meetings with local curators or magazine editors poring over spread layouts.

CAIRNGORM COFFEE

Map 2; 41A Frederick Street, New Town; ///stored.video.than;
www.cairngormcoffee.com

Bringing a little bit of Scotland's great outdoors to the heart of the New Town, this community-centric café and roastery is a staple on the local coffee scene. Step down into the welcoming natural wood-panelled basement bothy and you'll find perfectly brewed coffee, plus some seriously stylish outdoor merch. Don a Cairngorm hoodie and expect approving looks from local outdoorsy types who covet this gear like it's their favourite band tee.

» Don't leave without ordering one of the famous grilled cheese toasties with chilli jam for lunch (or elevenses, if you can't wait).

ARTISAN ROAST

Map 3; 57 Broughton Street, Broughton; ///duck.buck.stick;
www.artisanroast.co.uk

On entering this coffee shop and roastery and you'll be greeted by smiling baristas and a bohemian crowd of locals enjoying their daily pick-me-up. The snug, hessian-clad back room of the Broughton Street branch is the perfect spot to hide out for the afternoon, whether you need to check your emails or simply lose yourself in a good book.

Solo, Pair, Crowd

Coffee should be shared with friends, lovers or the characters in your latest favourite novel.

FLYING SOLO
Sips of inspiration

Penning your own novel? Grab an Italian dark roast at August_21 and get cracking. Enjoy encouraging vibes from the friendly staff upstairs, or descend to the basement for some serious solo writing.

IN A PAIR
Cosy coffee nook

For cultured chats with chums, grab a plush velvet chair at OQO. Cosy, Art Deco glam and open late, this place has a charming salon feel and Leith Walk locals, tourists and students all pile in.

FOR A CROWD
Medicinal meets

For a big group get-together, reserve a spot in the roomy basement of Black Medicine. Edinburgh locals swear by its caffeinated concoctions. Perfect for catching up the morning after the night before.

LITTLE FITZROY
Map 3; 46 Easter Road, Abbeyhill;
///deep.elder.slices; www.littlefitzroy.coffee

The dogs of Easter Road and their humans queue up for their daily cup of caffeinated goodness at Little Fitzroy. Championing local suppliers, pouring real Australian flat whites and blasting feminist punk rock from retro speakers, this place is a local obsession. Do as the sticker on the door says and support your local bad b****.

CULT
Map 5; 104 Buccleuch Street, Newington;
///heavy.hope.will; www.cult-espresso.com

The chalkboard outside this geek-chic coffee cave assures passersby that it's "not actually a cult", but coffee is a religion here. Inside shelves are crammed with comic books and model starships fly overhead, while the silver glint of laptops adds to the intergalactic vibe.

MODERN STANDARD COFFEE
Map 5; 49 Barclay Place, Bruntsfield; ///cups.shaped.still;
www.modernstandardcoffee.co.uk

Sick of being judged for her "basic" coffee preferences during her Edinburgh Uni days, Lynsey dreamed of opening up her own coffee shop that would be free of judgment or pretence. And she succeed: this has to be the most welcoming coffee shop in the city.

» Don't leave without sampling guest roasts based on the season (and sometimes the rugby) and tempting bakes from local suppliers.

The Local

Ah, the local. The cornerstones of the community, these classic pubs and beloved boozers are where regulars come together to have a good old blether over a pint or a dram and set the world to rights.

CARRIERS QUARTERS

Map 4; 42 Bernard Street, Leith;

///baked.curving.crest; www.carriersquarters.co.uk

Loud, unruly, and always a laugh, this is Leith's oldest pub. Ceilings are low (mind your head), windows are steamy, and loyal regulars love nothing more than to indulge in a bit of friendly banter with, well, just about anyone who'll listen really (you've been warned).

THE BARONY

Map 3; 81 Broughton Street, New Town;

///basis.remain.usage; www.thebarony.co.uk

Bohemian Broughton Street has its fair share of great drinking spots, but the Barony is the locals' choice. With a gorgeous wooden bar, open fireplaces, original Victorian features and a great selection of drinks, this quaint wee pub is perfect for a pint with pals or a quiet glass of red (the Carmenère is to die for).

THE CAMBRIDGE BAR

Map 2; 20 Young Street, New Town; ///really.slick.jams;
www.thecambridgebar.co.uk

Old-fashioned streetlights frame the entrance to this beloved
backstreet pub and, beckoned by the open hearth, a constant
stream of punters pour in to escape those cold winter nights. Join
them by the fire and choose from a range of guest beers.

» Don't leave without perusing the Cambridge's gourmet burger
menu. You're missing a trick if you don't order a side of cajun fries.

BENNETS BAR

Map 5; 8 Leven Street, Tollcross;
///candle.amber.emerge; www.bennetsbar.co.uk

This old-school boozer is an alluring world of warm dark wood,
ornate mirrors, stained glass and red leather. Plonk yourself down at
a wobbly, coaster-clad table and you'll find yourself among a merry
mishmash of students, suits and animated Tollcross regulars.

A true locals' hangout, the Star
Bar *(www.starbar.co.uk)* is tucked
away from view on a cobbled
New Town backstreet. This
cosy, kitsch, loosely Star Wars-
themed and wonderfully
understated dive bar has a
jukebox, beer garden, table
football and bags of character.
Oh yeah, and there's a skull in
the cellar (we'll let the bar staff
fill you in on that one).

ABODE BAR

Map 4; 229 Leith Walk, Leith; ///rock.shows.wacky; 0131 553 5900

Locals come to Abode for great chat and quality tipples, both of which
are served in abundance. Best mates and joint owners Nathan and
Louise have effectively turned this pub into Leith's very own living
room and the locals have made themselves right at home.

THE ANTIQUARY

Map 2; 72 St Stephen Street, Stockbridge;
///heavy.hooked.jelly; www.theantiquarybar.co.uk

Known to Stockbridge locals as the Tick, this is a proper local's local.
Expect regular folk nights, lively pub quizzes and sports on big game
days. Low wooden-beamed ceilings and a maze of hidden nooks give
the place a rural country pub feel – perfect for lazy afternoon pints.

NAUTICUS

Map 4; 142 Duke Street, Leith;
///slate.groom.couch; www.nauticus.co.uk

Everything in Nauticus tells a story. Embark on a boozy voyage of
discovery and learn about Leith's historical ties to ancient spice routes,
the wine trade and the whisky boom as you flick through a chaptered
menu of local craft brews, smoky single malts and gins old and new.
Drink in the curtained, lamplit Library Room next to the bar's piano,
or grab a seat near the open fire at the front and soak it all in.

» **Don't leave without** trying a cocktail. Nauticus co-founder Iain
McPherson is the brains behind some of Scotland's best cocktail bars.

Liked by the locals

"We've tried to make Abode a home from home, somewhere that is really part of the community. We choose local suppliers and produce whenever we can and our drinks lists are carefully considered."

NATHAN RYDER-JONES,
CO-OWNER OF ABODE BAR

AlFresco Tipples

*Drinking outdoors in Edinburgh is something of a
novelty, so of course it's done with great enthusiasm.
At the first sign of sun, locals flock to their nearest beer
garden or pub terrace to soak up those sweet rays.*

THE CUMBERLAND BAR

Map 2; 1–3 Cumberland Street, New Town;
///punks.spend.window; www.cumberlandbar.co.uk

For village-pub vibes, head straight for the Cumberland — and fast
if you want to nab a table. Here, just below street level, a weeping
willow offers welcome shade to a cluster of picnic benches nestled
beneath its rustling branches. Join the sunny Saturday crowd for a
refreshing cider and epic pub grub in this glorious green space.

THE PEAR TREE

Map 5; 38 West Nicolson Street, Newington;
///data.alive.regard; www.peartreeedinburgh.co.uk

When the first day of summer arrives, students and sports fans flock
to the Pear Tree in their droves, quickly filling what is easily one of
the biggest beer gardens in the city. Grab a drink from the indoor
bar and embrace the beer-fuelled revelry as you squeeze onto the

 To enjoy match-day vibes, visit when the Six Nations rugby tournament is shown on the big screens.

end of one of the long communal tables which sit below strings of twinkling festoon lights. There might even be a BBQ on the go (weather permitting of course).

TEUCHTERS LANDING

Map 4; 1C Dock Place, Leith;
///gears.frogs.email; www.teuchtersbar.co.uk

Is there anything better than sipping a pint by the water? We think not. Teuchters is a popular spot among Leith locals and their mates, who come here to while away sunny afternoons. Tables are usually packed with rowdy groups catching up on the latest goss, sipping on ice-cold beers, scoffing hearty Scottish pub fare and sharing stories to the sound of water lapping against the pontoon. Idyllic.

» Don't leave without ordering from the mug menu. Macaroni cheese and chips in a giant mug somehow makes everything better.

COLD TOWN HOUSE

Map 2; 4 Grassmarket, Old Town;
///buzz.oppose.parks; www.coldtownhouse.co.uk

This converted-church-turned-microbrewery beneath Edinburgh Castle is draped in flowers, bringing eternal spring to the Grassmarket. And it's just as elaborate inside, with themed rooms on every floor. But it's the rooftop terrace that steals the show: here you'll find gondola seats, blankets, a fire pit and a vintage Nissan van that doubles as a bar. Book a spot for sunset to catch the castle in its best light.

THE BLACKBIRD

Map 5; 37–39 Leven Street, Tollcross;

///soaks.behind.hope; www.theblackbirdedinburgh.co.uk

A bright orange bicycle above the door is your first clue: someplace wonderful lies beyond this otherwise unassuming entryway. Venture through the Blackbird's stylish interior and you'll find yourself in a secret drinking garden complete with outdoor heaters, blankets and quirky art installations. With the King's Theatre just up the road, this place has become the unofficial HQ for a young theatrical crowd who fit right in to such whimsical surroundings.

THE ROYAL DICK

Map 5; 1 Summerhall Place, Newington;

///discrepancy.sake.smug; 0131 560 1572

There's something hugely comforting about the Royal Dick. Yes uber-cool Summerhall is all about cutting-edge creativity, but this classic boozer – based in an old veterinary college – still stands strong. It's got cosy rooms and hearty pub grub, but the real draw?

Try it!
SPEAK UP

The Royal Dick hosts themed spoken word nights on the second Wednesday of each month – share your slam poetry with the crowd and earn yourself a free drink and a bite to eat (*www.fthorsesmouth.com*).

Its leafy lamplit courtyard, the best seat in the house to nurse a cold pint of Barney's IPA – did we mention it's brewed on-site?

>> Don't leave without checking out Pickering's gin distillery *(p82)* next door and sampling its classic G&T garnished with pink grapefruit.

ROSE STREET GARDEN

Map 3; 14 George Street, New Town;
///pack.middle.stroke, www.rosestreetgarden.com

Bid farewell to the mundane as you enter this stylized garden complete with outdoor cocktail bar, perfectly manicured lawn (artificial grass, of course) and swanky lounge seating. George Street lovelies sip on white wine spritzers, suited sophisticates tuck in to boozy Bloody Marys and a young fashion-conscious crowd make a beeline for the oh-so-photogenic floral arches to nab that perfect selfie.

THE OUTHOUSE

Map 3; 12A Broughton Street Lane, Broughton;
///gaps.slang.guess; 0131 557 6668

We'll be honest with you, finding a seat in the sun in Edinburgh can prove tricky at the best of times – which is why Broughton Street locals are hesitant to shout too loud about The Outhouse. But when it comes to off-beat outdoor drinking spots, this hidden pub is arguably one of the city's best-kept secrets. And we're letting you in on it. Expect bargain drinks, a vegan-friendly BBQ, zany art displays and even some local live music – plus that all important sunkissed beer garden.

Wine Bars

It may not be the first thing that springs to mind, but wine bars are a big thing in Edinburgh. These elegant spots are favourites among post-work professionals and late-night crowds.

TOAST

Map 4; 65 Shore, Leith; ///mimic.skin.assets;
www.toastleith.co.uk

Uber-chic Toast is whatever you need it to be, but if you happen to need a sophisticated wine bar that serves over 30 varieties of wine by the glass, you've hit the jackpot. Floor-to-ceiling windows flood the interior with natural light, making this the ideal place for a daytime catch-up with old friends over a tipple.

Shh!

After a long day shopping, savvy wine-lovers veer off Stockbridge's main drag and head straight through the doors of Good Brothers *(www.goodbrothers. co.uk)* to sip natural wines made by up-and-coming producers in some pretty surprising locations. Who knew they made wine in Scotland, eh?

SMITH & GERTRUDE

Map 2; 26 Hamilton Place, Stockbridge;
///bigger.erase.nods; www.smithandgertrude.com

This suave Stockbridge establishment is a celebration of life's simple pleasures. And what greater pleasure is there than wine and cheese? With an impressive menu of occasion-worthy wines to suit all budgets, plus a great selection of cheeses to match, you could do a lot worse than an evening at Smith and Gertrude.

THE DEVIL'S ADVOCATE

Map 1; 9 Advocate's Close, Old Town;
///plot.silly.talent; www.devilsadvocateedinburgh.co.uk

The exposed stone walls, candlelit mezzanine and slick service make this the ultimate spot to splash out on a fancy bottle for date night. Pair your choice with a charcuterie board or smoked fish sharing platter and enjoy a romantic evening in the heart of Edinburgh's Old Town.

» Don't leave without perusing the whisky menu – there are over 300 different varieties on offer. Staff will happily recommend a few.

PICKLES

Map 3; 60 Broughton Street, Broughton;
///dairy.curvy.survey; www.getpickled.co.uk

Big glasses of crowd-pleasing plonk, generous cheeseboards and a warm-hearted welcome from long-time owner Johnny – it's no wonder locals love Pickles. Wooden benches are always packed with rowdy rabbles of pals, who leave rather tipsy and very full.

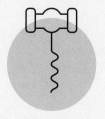

Liked by the locals

"At Bon Vivant, you feel like
you could be in the company of
bohemian libertines of days gone
by. Drinks with fellow writers feel
elevated, memorable
and noteworthy."

SIOBHAN HANLIN,
LOCAL AUTHOR AND BON VIVANT REGULAR

BON VIVANT

Map 2; 55 Thistle Street, New Town;
///bricks.descended.wide; www.bonvivantedinburgh.co.uk

Parisian literary salon meets proper pub at Bon Vivant, the perfect spot
in the city for writers' drinks. Rock up in the afternoon to do some
journaling; return at night when it's busy with a creative crowd and
slide into an old leather armchair for the ultimate in laid-back luxury.

THE CHAUMER

Map 2; 61 Queen Street, New Town;
///breath.sushi.noises; www.thechaumer.com

A vision in tweed and teal, the Chaumer's stylized interior feels almost
too polished for the public, but you don't need a VIP pass for entry.
Step through the door and let this oh-so-civilized tea room and wine
bar transport you to a time gone by where well-dressed couples swirl
glasses of Bourgogne Blanc and graze on Scottish charcuterie.
» Don't leave without checking out the Chaumer's "Enlightenment
Evenings", where a fine supper is accompanied by inspiring speakers.

ECCO VINO

Map 1; 19 Cockburn Street, Old Town;
///thank.dice.weds; www.eccovinoedinburgh.com

Drinking out front at Ecco Vino feels positively continental: think
winding cobbled streets, energetic buskers and bright summer
evenings (sun not guaranteed). Join the after-work crowd for a cold
glass of Sauvignon Blanc and nibble antipasti until closing time.

Cocktail Joints

Edinburgh's cocktail scene is thriving thanks to creative mixologists stirring things up – literally. Tempting locals to forgo the usual pint of Tennent's are fruity concoctions and laidback lounges to sip them in.

TIGERLILY

Map 2; 125 George Street, New Town;
///voices.charge.hints; www.tigerlilyedinburgh.co.uk

This deliciously decadent spot is the place to see and be seen. With bold, opulent prints from floor to ceiling, mirrored walls, plush velvet booths and outdoor tables that spill onto George Street's elegant pavements in summer, Tigerlily is just as glam as its well-heeled clientele. Add to that pages of cocktail masterpieces – and many

Try it!
MASTER MIXOLOGY

Aspiring mixologist? Sign up for a cocktail masterclass at the Voodoo Rooms *(www. thevoodoorooms.com)*. In just a few hours you'll have mastered (and sampled) classic cocktail recipes to try out at home.

Continue the party after closing time at Tigerlily's equally opulent sister club Lulu's, just downstairs.

a mocktail – and you're onto a winner. Feeling particularly extravagant? Book the After Dark private dining option to enjoy a speakeasy feel without the queues.

HOOT THE REDEEMER

Map 2; 7 Hanover Street, New Town;
///affair.shins.stump; www.hoottheredeemer.com

Hoot might look unassuming from the outside, but cross the threshold and you'll enter a vintage New Orleans funfair. We're talking an ice cream parlour, classic arcade games and tarot-inspired cocktails, plus a few surprises such as the highly quaffable "taps aff" – it's also a cheeky nod to the locals' inclination to remove their tops at even the slightest glimmer of sunshine. Try a cocktail slushie from the bar's very own slushie machine because, well, why not?

» Don't leave without grabbing yourself a boozy treat from Hoot's very own Señor Scoop. Espresso martini ice cream, anyone?

UNDER THE STAIRS

Map 1; 3A Merchant Street, Old Town;
///cube.locked.friday; www.underthestairs.org

Classy, cosy and understated, this little-known candlelit basement bar is the perfect spot for a romantic cocktail date. Pop in for one and, providing you hit it off, you'll emerge blinking into the street lights a few hours later after discovering boozy ingredients you never knew existed and spirits you didn't know you liked.

PANDA & SONS

Map 2; 79 Queen Street, New Town; ///navy.city.taking;
www.pandaandsons

The city's coolest cocktail joint takes the form of a humble barbershop.
And having been known to attract the odd lost soul in search of a
trim, Panda's disguise is pretty convincing. Like going into an old
Prohibition speakeasy, enter through a concealed door that doubles
as a bookcase, head down the stairs and step into a world of revelry.

BRAMBLE

Map 2; 16A Queen Street, New Town; ///guns.film.fund;
www.bramblebar.co.uk

It may not be obvious at first glance, but if you follow the stairs down
below street level you'll find yourself in the city's signature cocktail den.
Here elegant patrons sip creatively crafted concoctions that look way
too good to drink. Snap a pic for posterity – knowing full well that
you'll never quite do it justice – and raise a glass to the weekend
(no matter what day of the week it is).

THE LUCKY LIQUOR CO.

Map 2; 39A Queen Street, New Town; ///charm.fears.cats;
www.luckyliquorco.com

If Bramble is the grande dame of Edinburgh cocktails, Lucky Liquor
(run by the same owner) is the eccentric grandson. Ever changing
and always bang on trend, this concept cocktail bar reinvents its
menu every quarter, encouraging even the most daring of drinkers

to venture out of their comfort zone. Want to try something off menu? Ask nicely and Lucky's expert mixologists will whip up a custom concoction just for you – alcoholic or otherwise.

THE LAST WORD SALOON

Map 2; 44 St Stephen Street, Stockbridge;
///certified.text.riding; www.lastwordsaloon.com

The lighting is low and the mood is mellow at this local haunt, where Stockbridge sophisticates snuggle into their usual corners and sip on a selection of whisky cocktails. The walls are adorned with all sorts of weird and wonderful vintage paraphernalia, chesterfield armchairs abound, and there's even a toasty open fire, making this subterranean cocktail joint the perfect spot for a cheeky tipple on a chilly winter's eve.

» Don't leave without trying the saloon's namesake Last Word cocktail, a seriously drinkable concoction of gin, green chartreuse, maraschino liqueur and a squeeze of fresh lime.

THE COCKTAIL GEEKS

Map 1; Arch 14, 27 East Market Street, Old Town;
///games.yarn.noise; www.thecocktailgeeks.com

With a nod and a wink to cult classics (without any official affiliation) this place is a love letter to fandom. Shapeshifting every three months, Cocktail Geeks' immersive settings and themed libations invite you to drink in your favourite fantasy and sci-fi world. We won't name names, but previous iterations have included a famous schoolboy wizard, dinosaurs we thought were extinct and a certain lusted-after throne.

Breweries and Distilleries

There are award-winning craft breweries popping up all over the city – and with gin and whisky distilleries following suit, there's no shortage of options for those who like their tipples hyper-local.

CAMPERVAN BREWERY

Map 4; 112 Jane Street, Bonnington;
///crazy.tulip.sticks; www.campervanbrewery.com

The vibe here is seriously chilled, which isn't surprising given the owner is a beer-brewing surfer dude. Set in a pretty unremarkable industrial estate in Bonnington (the not yet gentrified bit of Leith), this beloved

Run by the team at Campervan, Lost in Leith Bar & Fermenteria *(0131 378 7834)* is home to the UK's first on-site barrel-ageing project. Check out the three barrels working their magic at the far end of the bar. Now it's just a case of waiting patiently.

brewery and taproom will give you all the local community feels; punters shuffle up to make space, dogs obligingly let you tickle their tummies and the person who'll pull your pint of "Leith juice" or "hoppy botanist" most likely brewed it too.

PORT OF LEITH DISTILLERY

Map 4; 53 Tower Street, Leith;
///window.they.sculpture; www.leithdistillery.com

While their main venue is still under construction and the first batch of whisky still ageing, the team at Port of Leith are busying themselves by making gin, port and sherry. Pop along to one of the tastings at the Stillhouse and expect great chat and fabulous gin cocktails in a down-to-earth industrial setting.

BARNEY'S BEER

Map 5; 1 Summerhall Place, Newington;
///epic.doctor.learn; www.barneysbeer.co.uk

Every beer-loving local is well acquainted with this revered Edinburgh institution. The classic beers are classics for a reason, but you'd be daft not to sample some of the more unusual brews made here, like the Lemon and Raspberry Radler, Marshmallow Milk Stout or, if you're into your sours, the tantalizingly tart tongue-twister Cosmic Ripple. Take a tour and tasting and finish up in the courtyard bar of the Royal Dick (p70), where you'll find Barney's flagship Volcano IPA on tap.

» **Don't leave without** trying Barney's eye-widening Sherbet Sour Pale. It'll make you question everything you know about beer.

PICKERING'S GIN

Map 5; 1 Summerhall Place, Newington; ///epic.doctor.learn;
www.pickeringsgin.com

Self-proclaimed botanical engineers Marcus Pickering and Matt Gammell founded Pickering's without any distilling experience. Nor did they have a distillery. But they did have a secret recipe scribbled on an old scrap of paper dated 1947. Today the secret's out, and every gin-loving Edinburger has sampled their botanical concoctions.

» Don't leave without checking out the latest eclectic exhibition in Summerhall's expertly curated gallery space next door *(p132)*.

BELLFIELD BREWERY

Map 6; 46 Stanley Place, Abbeyhill; ///format.taxi.basis;
www.bellfieldbrewery.com

The UK's first dedicated gluten-free brewery, Bellfield makes great beer that everyone can enjoy. Grab the latest session ale, a Lawless Village IPA or whatever experimental brew they've got on tap and catch up with pals in the relaxed taproom and beer garden.

EDINBURGH BEER FACTORY

Map 6; 32 Bankhead Drive, Sighthill; ///warm.dices.hired;
www.edinburghbeerfactory.co.uk

For beer lovers with a penchant for label art, Edinburgh Beer Factory is worth the trip. The Paolozzi lager is named in honour of Leith-born Pop Art pioneer Sir Eduardo Paolozzi, so it's fitting that the artwork across EBF's range of brews is some of the most eccentric around.

THE HANGING BAT

Map 2; 133 Lothian Road, Tollcross;
///lonely.takes.rips; www.thehangingbat.com

The Hanging Bat is the hangout of choice among locals who know their lambics from their goses and their porters from their stouts. Staff will happily chat you through the ever-changing chalkboard menu, and they may even let you peek into the Bat's very own (extremely micro) microbrewery to see what they're brewing up.

HOLYROOD DISTILLERY

Map 5; 19 St Leonard's Lane, Newington;
///lung.soaks.guilty; www.holyrooddistillery.co.uk

You'll smell the malty goodness long before you set eyes on this old railway building at the foot of Arthur's Seat. Holyrood became Edinburgh's first new single malt distillery in almost 100 years when it opened in 2019. Fact-filled sensory tours allow you to get hands-on with the ingredients and the equipment used to make its whiskies and gins. Oh, and there are a fair few samples to be had too.

Try it!
WHISKY MASTERCLASS

Take Holyrood Distillery's two-hour whisky masterclass led by head distiller and astrophysicist Jack Mayo. You'll learn all about the science of distillation, whisky production and the universe in general.

An afternoon of gin in
the city centre

A wee dram of whisky may well be Scotland's favourite tipple, but these days it's all about gin, glorious gin. While they wait for the aging process to work its magic, savvy whisky distillers are using their empty stills to create an equally delicious libation which is significantly quicker to produce – yup, you guessed it, gin. Learn all about its history and production in Scotland and sample some of Edinburgh's finest botanicals on this spirited city-centre adventure.

1. Sip Antics Gin School
1–3 Cumberland Street, New Town; www.sipantics.com
///form.note.fuel

2. Edinburgh Gin Distillery
1A Rutland Place, West End; www.edinburghgin.com
///energetic.wooden.rails

3. 56 North
2 West Crosscauseway, Newington; www.fiftysix north.co.uk
///curry.filled.spring

4. Pickering's Gin
1 Summerhall Place, Newington; www.pickerings gin.com
///epic.doctor.learn

📍 **Holyrood Distillery** ///lung.soaks.guilty

📍 **The Vennel** ///hurry.assets.necks

STOCKBRIDGE

QUEENSFERRY ST

WEST END **2**

LOTHIAN ROAD

Make your own gin at EDINBURGH GIN DISTILLERY
Head over to the Edinburgh Gin Distillery & Visitor Centre and make your very own one-off custom gin to take home with you. You can impress the staff with all the facts you learned at Sip Antics while you're at it.

BRUNTSFIELD

BROUGHTON

0 metres   400

0 yards   400

1 Learn the trade at
SIP ANTICS GIN SCHOOL

Start your gin-infused day at Sip Antics
Gin School at the Cumberland Bar
and learn all about the history of this
much-loved tipple.

DUNDAS STREET

JEEN STREET

GEORGE STREET

Regent
Gardens

REGENT ROAD

NEW TOWN

PRINCES STREET

NORTH BRIDGE

CANONGATE

Princes Street
Gardens

*Following the route of
the old Flodden Wall
that once marked the
city limits, **the Vennel** is
a handy shortcut with
great castle views.*

HOLYROOD ROAD

Edinburgh
Castle

ING'S STABLES ROAD

VENNEL

Pull up a stool at
56 NORTH

Saunter into student territory
to attend this trendy bar's
Scottish gin and cheese
masterclass. Stick to gin or try
a "recovery smoothie" if you're
in need of a wee pick-me-up.

LAURISTON PLACE

GEORGE SQUARE

3

University of
Edinburgh

BUCCLEUCH ST

SOUTHSIDE

The Meadows

MELVILLE DRIVE

Finish up at
PICKERING'S GIN

Tour the distillery and sample its
award-winning gins before retiring to the
Royal Dick next door, where the pub grub is
filling and Pickering's is in no short supply.

4

*Established in 2019,
Holyrood Distillery
is Edinburgh's newest
distillery. Here both
gin and whisky are
produced.*

SHOP

Forget fast fashion and generic high street stores: locals love nothing more than scouting for vintage gems, celebrating local designers and stocking up on gourmet treats.

Vintage Gems

*Never ones to follow the crowd, thrifty Edinburgers
will choose pre-loved over fast fashion any day. Have
a rummage in the city's best second-hand haunts and
you might just find yourself a one-of-a-kind piece.*

GODIVA BOUTIQUE

**Map 2; 9 West Port, Old Town; ///strain.formed.client;
www.godivaboutique.co.uk**

Designer wear in the front and vintage finds in the back, what brings
Godiva's collection together is a strong focus on sustainability – oh,
and a badass aesthetic to match. Owner Fleur MacIntosh channels
her inner Lady Godiva (whose fuchsia silhouette can be seen riding a
horned zebra on the wall) to fight the good fight against what she
calls "the soul-sucking monotony of fast fashion". Good on you, lass.

ARMSTRONGS VINTAGE

**Map 1; 83 Grassmarket, Old Town;
///mouse.during.party; www.armstrongsvintage.co.uk**

The signature red front of this vintage chain can be spotted at
numerous branches about town, but this Grassmarket flagship is
the biggest and most theatrical of all. Mannequins kitted out in

fedoras and bold-printed petticoats usher you inside, where, exploding from antique trunks and squeezed into floor-to-ceiling rails, you'll find second- (or third- or fourth-) hand bomber jackets, bridal dresses, more denim than you could ever imagine, and all the accessories to match.

MISS BIZIO COUTURE
Map 2; 41 St Stephen Street, Stockbridge;
///frosted.friend.patrol; 07775 583675

Step into the complete sartorial history of one woman's wardrobe and prepare to be blown away by the many fabulous vintage pieces that fashion-savvy owner Joanna Black has amassed over the years. And that's just scratching the surface – her entire collection is way too big to fit in her tiny shop at any one time. Every piece of her rotating stock has a story, and Joanna likes to make sure that each of her beloved garments is going to a good home.

» Don't leave without trying a new look suggested by Miss Bizio. She has an eye for personal styling, and might dress you in something bold you wouldn't have considered.

Try it!
REPAIR NIGHTS

Don't chuck it; fix it! Pop by The Edinburgh Remakery (www.edinburghremakery.org.uk) on repair nights and the team will give you a hand at mending. It also offers workshops teaching you the skills to repair and reuse.

EPOCA

Map 3; 365 Leith Walk, Leith; ///report.meal.kings; www.epoca.uk

This neighbourhood obsession stocks modern-era vintage fashion that's a bit punk, a bit classic, and a whole lotta rock 'n' roll. Under the watchful eye of resident ragdoll cat Argo, the place is run by a stylish team whose smiles and rainbow rails brighten up Leith Walk. Pop in for a wee neb, get chatting to owners Diago and Elisa about their latest clothes shipment from Italy and you'll inevitably leave hours later with a whole new (old) wardrobe.

LITTLE BLUE DOOR VINTAGE

Map 1; 25 Candlemaker Row, Old Town; ///half.ports.curl; www.littlebluedoorvintage.com

Is it a shop or a party? A glittering disco ball, fairy lights and the most encouraging of hosts, it could go either way really. With their bold street wear and flowing floral dresses, sisters Áine and Aisling have got you covered; their tiny treasure trove of 80s and 90s vintage

Shh!

Some of the best finds are to be had in the city's charity shops; the trick is knowing just where to look. Thrifty locals head for affluent areas like Morningside *(p108)* and Stockbridge to rummage through well-stocked charity shops that are regularly stocked with designer labels. You never know what you'll find.

garb is full of throwback finds fit for any occasion. Add to that some surprisingly reasonable price tags and you'll soon see why local fashionistas adore this wee place.

THOSE WERE THE DAYS

Map 2; 28 St Stephen Street, Stockbridge; ///asserts.expands.lists;
www.thosewerethedaysvintage.com

This unusually tidy boutique makes for a surprisingly serene shopping experience. Spacious displays showcase an expertly curated collection of one-of-a kind women's and men's vintage fashions, jewellery and accessories from the 1920s and beyond. It's not really a surprise to hear that this place is a favourite among costume designers – vintage finds from Those Were the Days have made many a cameo in some pretty big movies and TV dramas over the years.

» Don't leave without checking out Those Were the Days' vintage bridal boutique just next door.

CARNIVÀLE VINTAGE

Map 2; 51 Bread Street, Tollcross; ///branded.field.pot;
www.vintageedinburgh.com

This sophisticated shop is home to a collection of dapper finds harking back to bygone eras. Carnivàle owner Rachel Coutts entices local fashionistas and vintage aficionados with her vast (and still growing) collection of 1950s prom dresses, lace gowns, faux fur coats and tweed suits, pocket squares and all. If you're shopping for a classy occasion or a smart do, get thee to the fitting room, stat.

Retro Records

Edinburgh's record stores are where music lovers sift through vinyl old and new. There's no better way to spend an afternoon – just don't be surprised if you end up in a debate about obscure B-sides.

ASSAI RECORDS

Map 2; 1 Grindlay Street, Old Town; ///fear.arch.hurry; www.assai.co.uk

New kids on the block Assai Records have quickly become integral to the city's music scene, thanks in no small part to their impressive roster of in-store live music events, particularly around Record Store Day. The latest intake of converts from the digital versus analogue debate head here for freshly squeezed indie releases to flesh out their growing collections. Assai also stocks turntables, posters, hoodies and the occasional limited-edition signed album.

VINYL VILLAINS

Map 3; 5 Elm Row, Greenside; ///tube.shuts.owners; www.vinylvillains.co.uk

This Aladdin's cave of a record store has been enticing Edinburgh's musos with its genre-spanning range of new and second-hand vinyl, rare collectibles and impressive array of band tees since the 1980s.

Not sure what you're after? Don't sweat it, these guys have got some pretty strong opinions on what constitutes "good" music and will be happy to impart their wisdom. Fortunately they've got great taste too.

» Don't leave without having a good old root around the bargain bins – you never know what you might find.

VOXBOX

Map 2; 21 St Stephen Street, Stockbridge; ///timing.pens.bleak; www.voxboxmusic.co.uk

This small but friendly shop is doing its bit to keep the quirkiness of Stockbridge's indies alive. Pop in for a mooch around the carefully curated front shop (side A), where you'll find some serious music fans deliberating over which excellent-condition blues, jazz and rock collectibles to take home. Head through to the more chaotic but oh-so-charming back room (side B) for a good old rummage through Vox's treasure trove of bargain finds at £1.50 a pop.

ELVIS SHAKESPEARE

Map 3; 347 Leith Walk, Leith; ///cheeks.care.chart; www.elvisshakespeare.com

There are worse ways to spend an hour (or three) than rummaging and ruminating with owner David Griffin over his two great joys in life: music and books. Specializing in punk, alternative rock, indie and dance, this place is packed with great musical finds and literary gems. Browse the rare book collection or pick up a couple of those classics that you haven't quite got round to reading yet (shh, we won't tell).

Liked by the locals

"I spend most of my crate-digging time in Underground Solu'shn. The range of records there is astounding and they're never short of a hot tip or ten."

CHRIS MURRAY, LOCAL DJ, RADIO PRESENTER
AND DEDICATED CRATE DIGGER

UNDERGROUND SOLU'SHN

Map 1; 9 Cockburn Street, Old Town; ///verbs.backed.ranch;
www.undergroundsolushn.com

Specializing in dance and electronic music, Underground Solu'shn
has been supplying audiophiles with new and pre-loved vinyl and
audio equipment for decades – ask any local DJ where they bought
their first pair of decks, and, misty-eyed, they'll tell you it was here.

BACKBEAT

Map 5; 31 East Crosscauseway, Newington;
///wing.they.hers; 0131 668 2666

Backbeat is quite possibly Edinburgh's most chaotic record shop;
the place is literally overflowing with second-hand stock that's
haphazardly (some might say perilously) stacked from floor to
ceiling. Be prepared for a friendly grilling on arrival, but eccentric
owner Darren will be able to find exactly what you're looking for with
surprising ease. It seems there's method to this madness after all.

GOOD VIBES

Map 4; 153 Constitution Street, Leith; ///swept.whites.offer

Bringing some serious 1970s California charm to Leith (if not the
sunshine) is this adorable neighbourhood record, book and general
cute stuff store. Run by husband and wife dream team Mike and
Fi (and Woodstock the dog), this cheerful wee shop is a welcome
antidote to the clutter and chaos usually associated with vinyl hunting.
And true to its name, good vibes are guaranteed.

Book Nooks

As UNESCO's first City of Literature, Edinburgh is home to more than its fair share of bookshops, old and new. Browse bookish hangouts and meet local booksellers keeping the city's literary tradition alive.

TOPPING & COMPANY

Map 3; 2 Blenheim Place, Greenside; ///orbit.quarrel.calls; www.toppingbooks.co.uk

This book shop is always busy with book-loving locals who pop in for a browse and decide to stick around. And why wouldn't they? With over 700,000 titles over two floors, towering bookcases embossed with gold lettering and sliding ladders for those tricky-to-reach top shelves, Topping exudes old-school charm by the bucketload. So go on, find yourself a cosy corner and enjoy a free brew with your latest read.

TYPEWRONGER BOOKS

Max 3; 4A Haddington Place, Greenside; ///smile.jumpy.lace; www.typewronger.com

A small but expertly curated selection of fiction, poetry, zines and, of course, vintage typewriters all have a home here. Typewronger's wonderfully charismatic owner Tom Hodges will most likely offer you a cuppa (or a glass of wine) and a good old blether about all things bookish. Be sure to stop by for monthly open mic-nights, potluck Thanksgiving dinners and mince pies at Christmas time.

» **Don't leave without** tweeting from Tom's 1984 Adler SE320 electronic typewriter. Just tweet @tweetwronger and use the hashtag #typethis to have your ramblings appear in ink before your very eyes.

PORTOBELLO BOOKSHOP

Map 6; 46 Portobello High Street, Portobello;
///large.thin.carry; www.theportobellobookshop.com

As bright and breezy as the beach out the back and stocking a bit of everything from fiction and non-fiction to indie mags, board games and cute stationery, Porty's new bookshop has quickly established itself as an important hub for the local community. Bibliophiles of all persuasions pop in to peruse the latest staff picks and to check out what author events are coming up. Swing by during the annual Portobello Book Festival in autumn if you can.

Shh!

Carry a book you're happy to part with at all times. Why? This city is reciprocal when it comes to its reading, and you never know when you'll come across a lending library. Locals trade in their well-thumbed tomes for others at The Filmhouse Café, Leo's Beanery, the Meadows Community Garden or one of many pop-up libraries that can be found throughout the city.

MCNAUGHTAN'S BOOKSHOP

**Map 3: 3A and 4A Haddington Place, Greenside;
///colleague.head.owners; www.mcnaughtans.co.uk**

If you're the kind of bibliophile who covets the aged, erudite scent only an old book can provide, look no further: you've made it to literary heaven. Scotland's oldest second-hand and antiquarian bookshop has hardly changed a bit since it was first established in 1957 – save the small addition of Typewronger Books *(p96)*, which now occupies McNaughtan's former adjoining gallery.

TILL'S BOOKSHOP

**Map 5; 1 Hope Park Crescent, Newington; ///hidden.help.start;
www.tillsbookshop.co.uk**

Come on in and warm your hands by the open fire or sit in the wee window nook overlooking the Meadows. They say you can tell a lot about a person from their bookshelf. Well, you're about to become well-acquainted with Southside locals by way of their second-hand reads, and fortunately for you, they're a discerning bunch.

Try it!
BOOKISH TOUR

Follow the footsteps of Edinburgh's great authors on the Edinburgh Literary Pub Tour *(www.edinburghliterarypubtour.co.uk)*. Expect a great combo of all things books, history and, of course, beverages.

ARMCHAIR BOOKS

Map 2; 72–4 West Port, Old Town; ///dish.maple.pint;
www.armchairbooks.co.uk

Wind your way through a maze of floor-to-ceiling shelves that groan under the weight of more rare and second-hand books than is really acceptable for such a small space. To make a purchase, you'll first have to find the bookseller (no easy task), whose nose will most likely be buried deep in the pages of a novel.

LIGHTHOUSE BOOKS

Map 5; 43–5 West Nicholson Street, Newington;
///proof.trails.penny; www.lighthousebookshop.com

Read. Think. Resist. That's the Lighthouse motto. Expect genres that challenge the status quo, such as queer fiction, feminism and anti-racism. You'll be greeted with a cup of tea to fuel your activism – lovely.
» Don't leave without checking out Lighthouse's pay-it-forward scheme. Stories and knowledge should be accessible to all, right enough.

SCOTTISH POETRY LIBRARY

Map 3; 5 Crichton's Close, Canongate; ///share.facing.voices;
www.scottishpoetrylibrary.org.uk

This library was built to get readers hooked on Scottish poetry through a varied programme of events and workshops that celebrate the power of the imagination. The on-site shop curates anthologies by poets from Scotland and beyond. Pick up some playful postcards for a pound and send them to your literary companions from afar.

Gourmet Treats

Every neighbourhood in Edinburgh seems to have a little shop where foodies go to treat themselves. This is all thanks to artisans who've spent years finessing their craft, and locals who lap it up.

EDWARD & IRWYN

Map 5; 416 Morningside Road, Morningside; ///drips.wage.taking;
www.edwardandirwyn.co.uk

Edward & Irwyn's self-proclaimed chocolate wizards and expert chocolatiers have honed a craft they clearly love, and the results are quite frankly delicious. Try a golden salted honey caramel, a fresh cream truffle, real honeycomb set in dark chocolate or, for any Potter-heads out there, a handmade chocolate frog.

I.J. MELLIS

Map 1; 30 Victoria Street, Old Town;
///gladiators.ground.sing; www.mellischeese.net

This family-run cheese mecca has sat at the top of locals' gourmet shopping list for years thanks to Iain and son Rory Mellis's cheesy expertise. An ever-changing selection of farmhouse and artisanal delights like creamy Brie de Meaux and Hebridean Blue fills the interior of this classic old-school deli, with wheels of the stuff hanging from the ceiling and piled high in the windows. Staff are generous with samples and encourage a nibble before committing, which is precisely why you'll always see folk hanging around the counter.

» Don't leave without signing up to I.J. Mellis's monthly cheese club for a selection of artisan cheeses delivered to your door every month.

TWELVE TRIANGLES

Map 4; 22 Easter Road, Abbeyhill; ///hoping.kinks.envy;
www.twelvetriangles.co.uk

Having started life as a humble bakery selling a few splendid loaves a day, Twelve Triangles now has four outfits in the city. The bread is still great, but now you can pair it with all sorts of gourmet goodies, like a jar of Twelve Ts' homemade sweet chilli jam (locals lust after the stuff). Fancy something sweet? Twelve Ts is infamous for pedalling the most outrageous pastries, doughnuts and "cruffins" around (that's a muffin crossed with a croissant, and yes, you need it in your life).

KARINE DELI

Map 5; 376 Morningside Road, Marchmont;
///abode.deflection.perky; www.karinedeli.com

You better get in line if you want to try the finest almond croissants in town. The best part? They're still warm – much like the welcome you'll receive from Karine and her staff. Get there early as they're usually gone by noon. Fancy a lie-in? Pick up one of Karine's luxury picnic hampers to tote to the Meadows on a sunny day.

VALVONA & CROLLA

Map 3; 19 Elm Row, Greenside; ///showed.images.rings;
www.valvonacrolla.co.uk

Over 100 years ago, the Crolla family arrived in Edinburgh from Italy. Their entrepreneurial spirit and passion for food resulted in Valvona & Crolla, the flagship delicatessen, café, wine merchant, grocery store and purveyor of fine ingredients that we all know and love today. V&C ship only the highest-quality products direct from the motherland: expect whole legs of Parma ham and prosciutto suspended from the ceiling, syrupy-sweet balsamic vinegar by the bucketload, tomatoes bursting with flavour, elixir-like olive oil in beautiful glass bottles and fresh pasta for days. But it's not just about the food. Something of a spiritual home to Edinburgh's Scots-Italian community since 1934, V&C's is a cultural institution – every year the on-site gift room and book shop is transformed into a mini theatre venue during the Edinburgh Festival Fringe in August.

» Don't leave without asking the friendly staff at the deli counter if there are any tastings or demonstrations going at the Caffè Bar.

STOCKBRIDGE MARKET

Map 2; Saunders Street, Stockbridge; ///pages.farmer.fight;
www.stockbridgemarket.com

Gathering some of Edinburgh's finest purveyors of artisanal produce, this foodie hotspot is the ultimate Sunday morning hangout. Join a discerning crowd as you browse the many mouthwatering treats on offer. Yogis swing by after class for vegan brownies and oat milk lattes to complete their weekly ritual and young families rock strollers

 Here on a Saturday? Check out Castle Terrace Market and you'll find many of the same great suppliers.

from side to side as they peruse the many pickles and preserves. After something more substantial? Join the line at the paella stand for a truly epic lunch.

EAST COAST CURED

Map 4; 3 Restalrig Road, Leith; ///pens.tests.ballots;
www.eastcoastcured.com

Using produce from Scottish farms only and preparing everything from scratch on site, this adorable wee shop is a must for any cured meat-lover. Husband and wife Steven and Susie set up shop in 2017, and have since won a bunch of awards for their Scottish charcuterie. Salami of all shapes and sizes adorn the windows, salty prosciutto is sliced paper thin on chunky wooden boards, and the shop is filled with all things smoked, cured and fermented. Perfect for a picnic lunch, or to team with an evening tipple.

THE MARSHMALLOW LADY

Map 3; 14 Rodney Street, Canonmills; ///tribes.improving.nurses;
www.themarshmallowlady.co.uk

Nicole (aka The Marshmallow Lady) has been filling an unusual gap in the market since she first opened her Canonmills shop in 2012. Beautifully presented, totally homemade and the best in wacky flavour combos – this is marshmallow like you've never had it before. Whether you go for blood orange, strawberry and white chocolate or lemon meringue, prepare for a sweet, sticky, oozy taste-sensation.

Scottish Design

There's a strong tradition of art and craftsmanship in Scotland, but that doesn't mean it's all old-fashioned tartan and tweed – Scottish designers are at the top of their game, and everyone in Edinburgh wants a piece.

THE TARTAN BLANKET CO.

Map 4; 170 Great Junction Street, Leith; ///bliss.muddy.skill; www.tartanblanketco.com

Whether it's used as an oversized scarf to keep out the wind, to wrap up a wee one asleep in the car or thrown over your sofa for curling up with a cuppa, the classic tartan blanket will never go out of style, period. And if you're in the market for one of these Scottish essentials, the Tartan Blanket Co. is a must. Owners Emma and Fergus reinvest

Try it!
PERFECT PRINTMAKING

Book a masterclass at Edinburgh Printmakers (*www.edinburghprintmakers.co.uk*) to learn the art of printmaking. This heritage studio space, where many local artists develop their craft, is the largest of its kind in Europe.

a percentage of their profits into the community and environmental causes. Not only that, their beautiful blankets and scarves are made from recycled wool and cashmere, carrying a simple, traditional design into the modern age.

SCOTTISH DESIGN EXCHANGE
Map 2; 51 George Street, New Town; ///only.each.stacks;
www.scottishdesignexchange.com

Something of a hybrid between a shop and gallery, this stylish space sells gorgeous handmade ceramics, prints, clothes, textiles, accessories and quirky homewares by up-and-coming artists and designers. Retail therapy is all the more satisfying when you know that your hard-earned cash is going straight to the makers, right? And with over 300 involved to date, you'll be spoiled for choice.

» Don't leave without checking out the "Meet the Artists" page on the SDX website to find out more about the artists represented in store.

LOGAN MALLOCH LTD
Map 4; 13 Leith Walk, Leith; ///dice.behave.needed;
www.loganmalloch.com

Founded by married duo Brian Malloch and Phil Logan, this shop displays all sorts of artsy bits and bobs by local makers in an airy, minimal space. But it's Brian and Phil's enthusiasm for local design that makes this place really special. Looking for a pressie for a pal? Or maybe just for yourself. Either way, you're in the right place. Be sure to have a wee chat, they've got some great stories these two.

TOTTY ROCKS

Map 5; 45–7 Barclay Place, Bruntsfield;
///taps.riches.animal; www.tottyrocks.co.uk

With sleek retro flair, Totty Rocks creates whimsical yet refined looks, both off the rail and made to measure. These one-of-a-kind classics are all about the perfect, tailored fit, making sharp silhouettes for suits, trousers, capes and feminine military jackets. Maybe a tartan wool trench ought to be a staple in everyone's wardrobe?

THE RED DOOR GALLERY

Map 1; 42 Victoria Street, Old Town;
///backs.wounds.spring; www.edinburghart.com

The go-to spot to pick up a birthday present for artsy pals, this art-meets-funky-Scottish-design store always has you leaving with a gift for yourself, too. As well as gorgeous prints (you'll notice a strong Scottish theme here) by local artists, lining the shelves are some seriously cute items you never knew you wanted, much less needed: crocheted cacti, high-end notebooks you'll never write in and brooches emblazoned with expletives in a deceptively delicate floral script.

ANTA SCOTLAND

Map 2; 117–19 George Street, New Town;
///lovely.deck.elbow; www.anta.co.uk

This high-end design utopia has all you'll need and more for your contemporary Scottish home. Everything from the carpet to the lamps to the hand-thrown mugs resting on the tartan cube – and yes, that tartan cube too — is for sale. Expect timeless homeware, sturdy stoneware, and even cookery books — handy if you're not quite sure what to serve up on that swanky new stoneware dinner set.

KESTIN

Map 4; 1 Customs Wharf, Leith;
///cotton.healthier.privately; www.kestin.co

Kestin Hare's simple yet stylish menswear pieces are designed for durability and built for everyday use. Each garment (locally designed and made, of course) tells a story, with colour palettes inspired by the seascapes of Fife and the mountain slopes of the Cairngorms. But they don't just look good; technical fabrics are designed to withstand Edinburgh's typically dreich and drizzly weather, too. Even if you don't buy anything, the space exudes style and is a joy to browse.

» Don't leave without visiting the design studio on the second floor to admire the craftsmanship involved in designing these pieces.

WALKER SLATER

Map 1; 16–20 Victoria Street, Grassmarket; ///coffee.ears.minds;
www.walkerslater.com

In Scotland's Western Isles, cheviot sheep are shorn, wool becomes yarn and that yarn is handwoven in the homes of islanders into Harris Tweed. Okay, we're simplifying it a bit. Generations of local know-how go into making the material behind Walker Slater's on-point tailoring. If you can't quite bring yourself to fork out for a full suit, maybe you'll be tempted by a dashing tweed collar for your pooch instead?

MORNINGSIDE ROAD

COLINTON ROAD

Rummage the racks at
SHELTER
Check out the front windows for the best vintage items, then dive inside to filter through the rest. If you don't find a bargain on the racks, you just might on the bookshelves.

1

ALBERT TERRACE

Bag a bargain at
CANCER RESEARCH
It might sound odd for a charity shop to be known for its trendy clothing, but this one is. Once you've picked up a new look, browse the pottery and ceramics.

MORNINGSIDE PLACE

2

3

Score some home touches at
BETHANY CHRISTIAN TRUST
It may be somewhat chaotic (there's furniture and bric-a-brac everywhere), but that's exactly why it's so popular – that and the fact that you can pick up cute homeware for pennies.

MORNINGSIDE

Find your next read at
OXFAM BOOKSHOP
Just you try leaving this place without a handful of new (old) books. Dig deep and you might even find yourself some first editions.

MORNINGSIDE ROAD

4

CANAAN LANE

With its wild west-style saloon, jail and cantina, this little lane, known as **Edinburgh's Wild West** *looks like the set of a cowboy movie.*

5

Go big on bling at
CHEST, HEART & STROKE
This place feels like an upmarket artisan boutique. Go for the jewellery, china and designer coats, stay to admire the stunning antique cash register.

Support a good cause at
THE OPEN DOOR CAFÉ
This volunteer-run neighbourhood café raises funds for activities for the elderly to prevent social isolation. And the cakes are scrummy.

6

CLUNY GARDENS

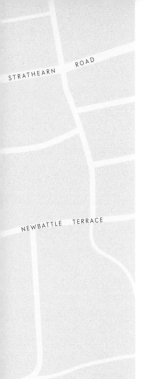

A thrifty afternoon in
Morningside

Known for its Victorian villas, private mansions and often parodied accent, Morningside is one of Edinburgh's more well-to-do neighbourhoods. Sure, upmarket boutiques are ten a penny round here, but thanks to the area's fashion-conscious residents, who update their wardrobe seasonally, the charity shops in this area are full of quality garments and some high-end designer surprises – all at bargain prices, of course.

1. Shelter
104 Morningside Road;
0131 447 8549
///plays.shots.extend

2. Cancer Research
87 Morningside Road;
0131 452 8064
///later.holly.papers

3. Bethany Christian Trust
93 Morningside Road;
0131 561 8997
///work.piles.moons

4. Oxfam Bookshop
210 Morningside Road;
0131 446 9169
///dwell.fakes.unable

5. Chest, Heart & Stroke
344 Morningside Road;
0131 447 6170
///snow.mash.labs

6. The Open Door Café
420 Morningside Road,
0131 447 9757
///shelf.sleepy.eager

📍 **Edinburgh's Wild West** ///backup.jacket.those

0 metres   200
0 yards   200

ARTS & CULTURE

Few cities can rival Edinburgh's thriving arts scene. The city may be famed for its summer festivals, but the performing arts take centre stage year-round.

City History

Edinburgh folk are proud of their city's history, which is woven into every close and cobbled street. Visit these historic spots to really get a sense of this place and its people, past and present.

EDINBURGH CASTLE

Map 2; Castlehill, Old Town; ///buck.ears.match; www.edinburghcastle.scot

It's an obvious one, but it's a biggie. Perched atop a volcanic crag, this ancient fortress is where the medieval city of Edinburgh began over a millennium ago, and the sense of history here is palpable. Walk in the footsteps of kings, queens, Scottish nobles and even pirates as you stroll up the Royal Mile to the Castle Esplanade. Even if you don't buy a ticket to the exhibitions inside (most locals don't), the views alone will leave you breathless. Or was that the hike up the hill to get here?

THE WRITERS' MUSEUM

Map 1; Lady Stair's Close, Old Town; ///worker.older.firms;
www.edinburghmuseums.org.uk/venue/writers-museum

Edinburgh's literary heritage runs deep, and the city has inspired many a writer over the years. This mansion-turned-museum celebrates the three giants of Scottish literature: Robert Burns, Sir Walter Scott and

Look out for the names of famous Scots writers engraved into the flagstones of nearby Makar's Court.

Robert Louis Stevenson. Check out the printing press that produced Scott's famous Waverley novels or peek at a rare plaster cast of Burns' skull, if that's what you're into.

MELVILLE MONUMENT
Map 3; 42 St Andrew Square, New Town;
///slime.passes.smooth

Leafy St Andrew Square may look innocent enough, but at its centre is a controversial monument honouring Sir Henry Dundas. Known as "The Great Tyrant" (the clue's in the name, really) Dundas frustrated efforts to abolish slavery, setting the movement back by 15 years. Meet here on Sunday afternoons for the Black History Walking Tour led by Lisa Williams, founder of the Edinburgh Caribbean Association, and learn about Edinburgh's connections with Africa, Asia and the Caribbean from Tudor times to the present day.

» Don't leave without reading the plaque rededicating the monument to the memory of those whose enslavement was prolonged by Dundas.

OLD CALTON CEMETERY
Map 3; Waterloo Place, Old Town; ///knee.shows.foil

The thought of ambling through a cemetery may give some people the creeps, but you'll be surprised to find many a local enjoying an afternoon ramble among the weathered gravestones of this ancient burial ground. Even more surprising is the statue of Abraham Lincoln atop the only Civil War memorial outside of North America.

THE PEOPLE'S STORY MUSEUM

Map 3; 116 Canongate, Old Town;
///fields.closer.later; www.edinburghmuseums.org.uk

Far from regaling royal histories, this down-to-earth museum shares the story of Edinburgh's working class. Young families explore the three floors of this old jailhouse to learn what life was like away from the pomp and ceremony of the castle, their wee tots entranced by life-size models that depict daily life from the 18th century to present day. Rotating exhibitions cover labour unions, the suffragettes, punk, football and the LGBTQ+ movement. But a common thread throughout is the abject poverty faced by many of the city's citizens, past and present – something that is too often forgotten in the glitz and glamour of this romanticized Festival city.

TRINITY HOUSE MARITIME MUSEUM

Map 4; 99 Kirkgate, Leith; ///fame.trying.monkey;
www.trinityhouseleith.org.uk

Obscured by the back of a somewhat uninspiring concrete shopping precinct, this hidden museum chronicles Leith's maritime history. Visits include a tour of the building and the weird, wonderful and downright bizarre nautical paraphernalia (octants, sextants and a giant narwhal tusk) that adorn its dusty interior. Compasses and charts are laid out across the grand Convening Room's 6-m (20-ft)- long table as if its seasoned seafarers have just nipped out for a tea break.

» Don't leave without popping to the loo. It seems a bit crass to say, but you're not going to want to miss the opportunity to spend a penny in this still functioning antique toilet.

ANATOMICAL MUSEUM

Map 1; Doorway 3, Medical School, Teviot Place, Southside;
///hiding.acting.tend; www.ed.ac.uk/visit/museums-galleries/anatomical

Step into the grand foyer of this university museum and you can't help but notice the elephant in the room. Well, two elephants actually. Their skeletons guard the entrance to this former world centre of anatomical research, where the likes of Charles Darwin and Arthur Conan Doyle studied. Today enthusiastic students gleefully escort wide-eyed visitors round a treasure trove of gory artifacts and preserved body parts.

THE WEE MUSEUM OF MEMORY

Map 4; Ocean Drive, Leith; ///grid.bells.yappy;
www.livingmemory.org.uk

Unlike most museums, this place encourages a hands-on approach to history. Each of the 10,000+ pleasantly familiar objects comes with a story, whether it's a 1930s school desk, a 1950s TV set or a genuine Tamagotchi – remember those? Don't worry if you don't, friendly staff are on hand to jog your memory (and offer copious amounts of tea).

Try it!
TOUR ON YOUR TIME

Download the Curious Edinburgh app *(www.curiousedinburgh.org)* for tours you can do on your own time: pick from Jewish history, India in Edinburgh, the BLM mural trail, a history of brewing and more.

Favourite Museums

Whether it's a dedicated visit or a rainy day activity, locals always make time to explore the latest exhibitions in these best-loved museums and galleries. And fortunately for them, there's plenty to choose from.

NATIONAL MUSEUM OF SCOTLAND

Map 1; Chambers Street, Old Town; ///beyond.home.joined; www.nms.ac.uk

Spread across four storeys and two wings (the "old bit" and the "new bit") are long-extinct species housed in glass cases, a T-Rex skeleton and ancient Egyptian coffins that give visitors the heebie-jeebies. Sure, during the day, young families rule the roost, but come nightfall, the museum is the domain of grown-ups. On the last Friday of the month

Edinburgh's museums own more objects than can be displayed at any one time. The overflow is stored (and restored) at the city's Museums Collections Centre *(www.nms.ac.uk)*. Here you'll find Roman busts, forgotten masterpieces and statues lumped together in a gloriously chaotic, uncurated space.

young professionals hit up the hugely popular museum Lates for an adults-only afterparty with fun events, live music, drinks and dancing – and thankfully no screaming bairns in sight.

» **Don't leave without** checking out the viewing terrace on the sixth floor for some panoramic views across the city's rooftops.

DYNAMIC EARTH

Map 3; Holyrood Road, Holyrood; ///clean.hung.issue;
www.dynamicearth.co.uk

Far from the stuffy displays and "no touching" policy of traditional museums, this interactive experience encourages visitors to get hands-on with the exhibits. Melt your fingertips into a giant ice cap, travel back to the beginning of time in the Deep Time Machine, explore the depths of the world's deepest oceans and journey across the universe at the speed of light. Documenting over 4 billion years of history may seem a bit ambitious. Well, it is. But it's also downright fascinating.

FRUITMARKET GALLERY

Map 1; 45 Market Street, Old Town; ///events.bake.future;
www.fruitmarket.co.uk

Coffee-in-hand commuters and travellers lugging wheelie suitcases always make time for a quick zoom around this wonderful wee gallery after stepping off their train. Hosting regularly changing exhibitions by contemporary Scottish and international artists, it's always worth popping in to see what's on. Swing by the café and bookshop and pick up a sugary treat and a good read to fuel your onward journey.

SCOTTISH NATIONAL GALLERY

Map 2; The Mound; ///beard.dice.tables; www.nationalgalleries.org

A national gallery may evoke images of highbrow critics and tourists wandering quiet halls, but here a vibrant young crowd adds to the mix. Join them as they enjoy a cultured lunch break and pontificate over a world-class collection by Scottish and European masters.

SURGEONS' HALL MUSEUMS

**Map 1; Nicolson Street, Old Town; ///shower.runs.fence;
www.museum.rcsed.ac.uk**

Preserved skin floating in jars, half-rotten skeletons and some very old human teeth – this place is definitely not for the fainthearted. With collections dating back to 1699, Surgeons' Hall was set up to teach anatomy to medical students, but they needed bodies. Enter Burke and Hare, the murderous duo who famously made a fortune providing fresh cadavers to the medical school, no questions asked. Well, until they were discovered and hanged in 1882, that is. Spot the noose marks on Burke's death mask, which is on display in the museum.

MUSEUM OF CHILDHOOD

**Map 1; 42 High Street, Royal Mile; ///bowls.game.hook;
www.edinburghmuseums.org.uk**

Every Edinburgh local remembers being taken around this time-capsule museum by their parents or teachers. Its charming collection of toys, books, clothes and games map the experiences of childhood from the 1800s to present day, and there's everything you can imagine (or remember). A 1970s Raleigh Chopper, Barbie dolls, a Nintendo 64, a Buzz Lightyear action figure – there's nothing like seeing your favourite toys in a museum to make you feel old, eh?

SCOTTISH NATIONAL GALLERIES OF MODERN ART

Map 6; 73 Belford Road, West End; ///rents.games.maps; www.nationalgalleries.org

Vast landscaped grounds dotted with sculptures, locals lounging on the grass and, above the colonnaded entrance, a reassuring message that "everything is going to be alright" in huge neon lettering: it's easy to see why Edinburgers love hanging out at this modern art complex. Spanning the gallery's two buildings (Modern One and Modern Two) you'll find works by big names like Matisse and Picasso alongside mind-bending interactive installations by up-and-coming artists.

» Don't leave without checking out the roster of art classes held at the Mods. Life drawing? Photography? Take your pick.

SCOTTISH NATIONAL PORTRAIT GALLERY

Map 3; 1 Queen Street, New Town; ///equal.fame.exam; www.nationalgalleries.org

One of the most spectacular buildings in Edinburgh, this red-stoned Gothic palace was the world's first ever purpose-built portrait gallery. The golden, glittering interior displays the faces of those most brave, influential or simply wealthy enough to have their portraits painted.

Film and Cinema

Sure, August's International Film Festival sees movie fans flock to the city. But the big screen is a must at any time of year. Rainy days call for a trip to the pictures, where hot, buttery popcorn and cult classics await.

THE FILMHOUSE

Map 2; 88 Lothian Road, West End; ///zeal.vanish.casino;
www.filmhousecinema.com

Home to the annual Edinburgh International Film Festival, this indie arthouse cinema is beloved by a fiercely loyal fanbase, who flock here year-round. Cinephiles and groups of pals convene in the café-bar to debate which of the Filmhouse's eclectic selection of world and indie titles to see next. Oh, and if you're here during the Film Festival, book ahead. Trust us, local bums fill these seats fast.

CAMEO PICTUREHOUSE

Map 5; 38 Home Street, Tollcross; ///finger.images.smashes;
www.picturehouses.com/cinema/the-cameo

The Cameo may be a bit battered around the edges, but with its classic lightbox lettering and plush red seats, it's managed to hold onto its charm over the years. And with a great selection of indie

 Check for the Cameo's dog-friendly showings. No dog? No problem. You'll be surrounded by puppy pals.

flicks and blockbusters, it's no wonder that many a local film buff is a Cameo diehard. Grab a glass of wine in the Cameo Bar and debrief with pals after the movie.

DOMINION CINEMA

Map 5; Newbattle Terrace, Morningside; ///supply.saying.stress; www.dominioncinema.co.uk

This family-run Art Deco movie theatre has been going strong since the 1940s. After work, young professionals come here to soak up the irresistible old-school vibe, where nothing is over-complicated and the smell of fresh popcorn wafts through the air. Go first class and sink yourself into the luxurious leather loveseat sofas (perfect for date night) and have your drinks order arrive during the film. When the credits start rolling, you'll wish you didn't have to leave.

BRASS MONKEY

Map 1; 14 Drummond Street, Old Town; ///ranged.track.hurry; www.brassmonkeyedinburgh.co.uk

Okay, it's not technically a cinema. But this quirky bar serves up all the cosy film-night feels – perfect for an afternoon snuggled up with your besties. The walls are plastered with vintage movie posters and informal screenings have been held in the cosy mattress room every afternoon since, well, longer than anyone can remember. No seats, no tickets, just loads of pillows and a daily tradition of cult classics from a seemingly endless in-house collection.

SCOTSMAN PICTUREHOUSE

Map 1; 20 North Bridge, Old Town; ///brief.tiger.flies;
www.scotsmanpicturehouse.co.uk

Feeling a wee bit fancy? Attached to the opulent Scotsman Hotel is the most luxurious and exclusive cinema in town. Seating just 48 in sumptuous leather armchairs, each with its own side table and classic empire lamp that gives off an elegant glow, this intimate venue is where locals go to catch a screening of their favourite time-honoured masterpiece. The impressive Art-Deco surrounds are a nice touch too. Book one of the dining packages and enjoy brunch, afternoon tea or a three-course candlelit dinner in the Scotsman's glittering restaurant before or after your showing. In short? This is dinner and a movie done right.

» Don't leave without checking out the Scotsman Steps. This public artwork by 2010 Turner Prize winner Martin Creed is not only beautiful, it also conveniently links North Bridge with Market Street below.

VUE OCEAN TERMINAL

Map 4; Ocean Drive, Victoria Dock, Leith;
///tested.lonely.sugar; www.myvue.com

A cinema chain may offer up harrowing flashbacks of sticky carpets, screaming kids and oh-so-outdated mainstream vibes, but this branch is a local fave thanks to its 12 massive screens and reclining leather seats for all (not just those who pay a VIP premium). Movie-goers flock here to see guilty-pleasure new releases and superhero flicks with a big bucket of popcorn or an overpriced bag of pick 'n' mix for a trusted good viewing. Sure, it's no arthouse indie, but it does the trick.

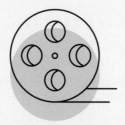

Liked by locals

"There's the Filmhouse, the Cameo and the Dominion. But for me nothing can beat VUE at Ocean Terminal for its cheap tickets, reclining seats and massive screens. The point is, there's a cinema to match any type of experience you're after."

ROSS SCOTT, EDINBURGH FILM-MAKER
AND SWEET AND SALTY POPCORN FAN

Performing Arts

Music, dance, theatre, comedy; Edinburgh is one of the world's greatest cities for performing arts. Edinburgh Festival and Fringe are highlights of course, but this city puts on one hell of a show year round.

THE LYCEUM

Map 2; 30B Grindlay Street, Old Town; ///ready.eager.scans, www.lyceum.org.uk

The lifeblood of Edinburgh's theatre legacy, the Lyceum is a prime producer of theatre and dance. This is your archetypal red curtain, crystal chandelier kinda place. Balancing classic and contemporary, home-grown and international, the Lyceum is a favourite for locals seeking a modern twist on an avant-garde piece during the summer line-up, and an elevated *Christmas Carol* in December.

TRAVERSE THEATRE

Map 2; 10 Cambridge Street, Old Town; ///large.impact.ever; www.traverse.co.uk

Sure, seasoned thespians adore the Trav, but with its strong emphasis on inclusiveness, diversity and young talent, this new writing venue is popular among first-time theatre-goers too. Also tempting newbies

Fringe of Colour *(www. fringeofcolour.co.uk)* champions productions by Black and under-represented artists.

through the doors is an easily digestible 50-minute performance accompanied by a hot pie and a refreshing beer. A play, a pie and a pint – perfection.

THE STAND COMEDY CLUB

Map 3; 5 York Place, New Town; ///ever.zoom.drip; www.thestand.co.uk

A loyal bunch of regulars keep this basement comedy club packed every night of the week. Seats are first-come, first-served, so if you dread getting picked out (and picked on), be sure to arrive early and stake out a spot at the back. Monday night improv is a particular fave, promising punters a fast, frantic and totally improvised show based on suggestions and heckles from the audience.

» Don't leave without ordering a heaped plate of nachos to your table to sustain you for hours of belly laughs.

FESTIVAL THEATRE

Map 1; 13–29 Nicholson Street, Old Town; ///inform.likes.crisis; www.capitaltheatres.com/your-visit/festival-theatre

No prizes for guessing that this place is the beating heart of Edinburgh Festival's theatre programming. Beyond the festival, theatre-goers climb the grand staircases to enjoy opera, ballet and touring West End shows from the vertiginous heights of Scotland's largest and most prestigious venue. And they usually arrive early to swan about the lavish balconies and enjoy a pre-theatre drink.

BEDLAM THEATRE

Map 1; 11B Bristo Place, Old Town; ///cape.lodge.update;
www.bedlamtheatre.co.uk

This Neo-Gothic church became the headquarters for the Edinburgh University Theatre Company in 1980. Located on the site of the old city poorhouse, its name is a reference to the city's first mental health hospital that once stood nearby. Now the oldest student-run venue in the UK, this 90-seater black box theatre offers a fresh take on just about any genre going. As well as weekly improv shows, the stage will host student opera one week and new writing the next. Yes, you can check what's on in advance, but where's the fun in that?

LEITH THEATRE

Map 4; 28–30 Ferry Road; Leith ///idea.piles.among;
www.leiththeatretrust.org

Leithers are delighted with the renovation of their once-abandoned music and theatre venue. There's a roguish, down-to-earth charm about the place, and having hosted many a big name in the past

Try it!
BREAK A LEG

Feeling inspired by what you've seen on stage? Book a dance class or pop along to a drop-in session at DanceBase *(www. dancebase.co.uk)* for one-off classes in everything from ballet to burlesque.

(AC/DC, Thin Lizzy and Kraftwerk), this Edinburgh International Festival venue continues to host great gigs and shows throughout the year; if you can catch a show here, do.

>> **Don't leave without** looking for the portrait of Mary Moriarty, legendary landlady of the Port O'Leith Bar, board member of Leith Festival and unofficially elected "Queen of Leith".

THE USHER HALL

Map 2; Lothian Road, Tollcross; ///list.repay.boat; www.usherhall.co.uk

The Usher Hall takes centre stage on Lothian Road, sandwiched between the Traverse and Lyceum like the crown jewel of this theatrical square. Seating over 2,000 people, the stately domed concert venue is said to have the best acoustics in all of Europe. And it's just as well: here you'll find concerts and events spanning a range of genres – classical, orchestral and choral, but also cream-of-the-crop rock, pop, blues and even big-name comedy.

CHURCH HILL THEATRE

Map 5; Morningside Road, Morningside; ///brief.snack.sports;
www.churchhilltheatre.co.uk

Fondly known as "the Churchy", this pink sandstone former church-turned-performing arts venue is where Edinburgh's theatre-lovers come to worship at the altar of AmDram (that's amateur dramatics, to the uninitiated). If you're in the area, make like a local and catch a community play or charming panto performance put on by local legends the Edinburgh People's Theatre. Oh yes you should!

Indie Galleries

Edinburgh's indie art scene is more than just the art itself. Indie galleries and creative studio spaces are all about supporting local makers, welcoming new faces and inspiring the creatives of tomorrow.

EMBASSY GALLERY

Map 3; 10B Broughton Street Lane, Broughton; ///verge.taxi.fence; www.embassygallery.org

Veer way off the beaten track of Edinburgh's established art scene and venture down a cobbled side lane to find this grassroots arts space where everything feels a bit DIY. Run entirely by volunteers, Embassy operates as a non-profit and, with strong ties to Edinburgh College of Art, it's the place in the city to check out works by early-career artists. This place is all about community – go show your support.

DOVECOT STUDIOS

Map 1; 10 Infirmary Street, Old Town; ///sticks.unions.affair; www.dovecotstudios.com

When Edinburgh's first Victorian bathhouse faced demolition in 1995, renowned tapestry firm Dovecot Studios stepped in to save the day. Fast forward to the present day and this breathtaking space is now one of the most happening creative spots in the city. Art-loving locals come for the exciting roster of cutting-edge tapestry exhibitions and events and end up staying for hours, totally captivated by the intricate work of master weavers. Who knew tapestry could be this cool, huh?

» Don't leave without swinging by Dovecot Studios' fab wee gallery shop to pick up some stunning locally made art and crafts.

COBURG HOUSE ART STUDIOS
Map 4; 15 Coburg Street, Leith; ///parts.launch.shut; www.coburghouse.co.uk

This former granary is a thriving hub for artists, designers and makers. The studios are occupied by a collective of over 80 creatives making all sorts of wonderful things (seafaring graphic novels, limited edition risoprints and statement unisex jewellery to name just a few). Keep an eye out for open-studio events for a peek behind the scenes. Feeling inspired? There are heaps of classes on offer here, from watercolour painting to hammering your own wedding rings.

If you know, you know. And if you don't, well you're about to find out. Ltd INK *(ltdinkcorporation. com)* is a contemporary art space in an old ambulance depot on Brunswick Street, just off Leith Walk. Visit for zany events, fascinating talks and off-the-wall exhibitions organized by a collective of esteemed (and some pretty eccentric) Scottish artists.

INGLEBY GALLERY

Map 3; 33 Barony Street, Broughton; ///action.round.handy;
www.inglebygallery.com

For two decades, directors Richard and Florence Ingleby have been thoughtfully exhibiting works by local and international contemporary artists at this swish Edinburgh gallery. Sure enough, art afficionados seeking their next cultural fix flock here in their droves, but you'll also find a quieter, more contemplative crowd. Past exhibitions include the imaginary island of Charles Avery in the Gates of Onomatopoeia and a series of mesmerizing glassworks made from recycled construction materials by acclaimed Edinburgh artist Kevin Harman.

STILLS

Map 1; 23 Cockburn Street, Old Town;
///times.flags.firmly; www.stills.org

Stills is Edinburgh's one-stop-shop for all things photographic. We're talking black-and-white stills, stunning landscapes, moody portraits and playful Polaroids. Yes, rotating exhibitions showcase the work of big names in the industry, but it's the talks and workshops that have earned this place its stellar reputation among a tight community of passionate photographers. A constant stream of shutterbugs pop in to develop film reels in the on-site dark room or attend artsy film screenings and lectures that ask the big questions. What is the optical unconscious? Can we ever really be subjective? Is film really dead? Ask anyone here and the answer will be a resounding no.

» Don't leave without browsing Stills' library of photography books – perfect for budding photographers looking to learn a thing or two.

FLAMINGOSAURUS REX

Map 5; 22 Bruntsfield Place, Bruntsfield; ///throw.paused.pest;
www.flamingosaurusrex.com

Quirky, fun (the clue's in the name) and full of energy, this welcoming
gallery and shop is a champion of up-and-coming artists, and a
stalwart of Bruntsfield's local community. Here you'll find bold prints,
locally designed crafts and a regular roster of dynamic exhibitions
that supportive pals, family and art lovers pack out without fail.

COLLECTIVE

Map 3; City Observatory, Calton Hill; ///beats.locate.couch;
www.collective-edinburgh.art

No longer used for stargazing and pondering the great unknown, the
old city observatory is now dedicated to observation of a more intro-
spective kind. The gallery brings people together to look at, think about
and produce contemporary art. The Satellites Programme supports
the next generation of creative minds and makers, while exhibitions,
guided walks, and fun events bring contemporary art to all.

Try it!
GET ARTY

The Art Club (www.artclubedinburgh.com)
hosts inclusive Paint and Wine evenings in
a bright and airy Canonmills studio. The
teachers are friendly and all are welcome,
so pick up that brush and get painting.

Creative Spaces

This city's a pro when it comes to integrating arts into community spaces. And we're not just talking about the Festival. Tap into Edinburgh's creative side at these fringiest of venues, with or without the main event.

SUMMERHALL

Map 5; 1 Summerhall, Newington; ///river.chest.lobby; www.summerhall.co.uk

Cultural institution and community hub, Summerhall is the ultimate spot to soak up creative vibes thanks to a reliably eclectic line-up of zany events that keep locals coming back for more. Where else in the city would you be able to catch comedy nights, attend artist talks, listen to post-punk disco-funk, boogie to Balkan beats and build your own synth machine, all under one roof?

THE PITT

Map 4; Pitt Street, Leith; ///accent.kicks.sticks; www.thepitt.co.uk;

Come the weekend, this unassuming warehouse and yard becomes Leith's place to be. Pals let loose at this buzzing street food market and events space, complete with live music and local DJs spinning decks, a bonfire (on chilly days), and locally brewed craft beer on tap. If you're looking for Edinburgh Festival vibes without the faff of trying (and failing) to avoid the crowds, you've hit the jackpot here.

CUSTOM LANE

Map 4; 1 Customs Wharf, Leith; ///door.normal.return; www.customlane.co

Part gallery, part events space, part art studio, Leith's old Customs House is today a dynamic community hub. Pop in for a wee mooch and you'll spot locals prepping DIY projects at the Edinburgh Tool Library and artists lugging canvases up and down stairs to their studios. Feeling inspired? The Lane hosts workshops on all sorts of crafts, from zine-making masterclasses to smoke-firing ceramics.

» Don't leave without checking out Talks at the Lane, a series of lectures and lively conversations around themes of design and making.

OUT OF THE BLUE DRILL HALL

Map 3; 36 Dalmeny Street, Leith; ///inform.camps.bring; www.outoftheblue.org.uk

Out of the Blue is behind all kinds of artsy goings on in the Burgh. The aim of this big-hearted community organization is to encourage locals to tap into their own creativity. And Edinburgers looking to flex their creative muscles are jumping at the chance, making use of the on-site recording studios, artists' ateliers, performance spaces, gig venues, quarterly arts fairs and monthly flea markets (well worth checking out if you're on the hunt for some locally made goodies).

Solo, Pair, Crowd

Whether you're exploring solo or looking for a group hang, Edinburgh's got enough quirky venues to keep you occupied for days.

FLYING SOLO

Get lost in a good story

Bringing literature to life, the Scottish Storytelling Centre is the place to go for theatre, talks, a hidden library and, of course, some great storytelling events. You'll quickly find yourself surrounded by fellow bookworms.

IN A PAIR

Get crafty with a pal

We Make Edinburgh is a great wee spot offering a range of creative workshops organized by the Edinburgh Craft Club. Catch up with a good pal and make some kick-ass kokedama.

FOR A CROWD

Live and loud at Leith Arches

Thanks to old pals Carmen Allison and Donna Howden, this once derelict space is now one of the city's coolest hangouts. Bring your mates and mingle with artists, musicians and lovely Leithy folk.

ST MARGARET'S HOUSE

Map 6; 151 London Road, Meadowbank; ///beside.traded.oils
www.edinburghpalette.co.uk/st-margarets-house

Social enterprise Edinburgh Pallette has given this neo-brutalist office block a whole new lease of life. Today, local creatives come together and collaborate in its warren of community arts spaces, studios, theatre venues, rehearsal rooms and several floors of gallery space.

SKETCHY BEATS CAFÉ

Map 4; 208 Great Junction Street, Leith;
///force.models.office; 07719 675217

What started life as a semi-regular life-drawing class has flourished into a small but spectacular not-for-profit arts café and event space. Expect live hip hop, spoken word, poetry slams, spontaneous jam sessions and heated debates. Oh, and life drawing too.

THE BISCUIT FACTORY

Map 4; 4 Anderson Place, Leith; ///raced.atomic.passes;
www.biscuitfactory.co.uk

A maze of exposed brickwork, poured concrete and iron beams, this former biscuit factory is probably the closest you'll get to a bit of Berlin in Edinburgh. Okay, so it might not be in the same league as Berghain, but catch a club night here and you're in for a treat; Mike Skinner and the Blessed Madonna are among the many esteemed BF DJ alumni.

» **Don't leave without** enjoying a cheeky tipple beneath the festoon lights in the outdoor lane bar. The atmosphere here is electric.

On the trail of
Edinburgh's haunted history

Edinburgh's ghoulish past is woven into the very fabric of the city, lurking not only in the gloomy closes of the Old Town, but in the hidden streets and ancient dwellings of the even older town that lies beneath it. Learn about the city's haunted history, from grizzly political murders that shaped the country's future to hangings, riots and diseases that once plagued its tightly packed tenement buildings. There's a dark side to Edinburgh; venture deeper, if you dare.

Dine in gothic style at THE WITCHERY BY THE CASTLE
Treat yourself to a magical candlelit dining experience in this opulent Gothic boutique hotel, once a 16th-century merchant's house.

1. Greyfriar's Kirkyard
26A Candlemaker Row;
www.greyfriarskirk.com
///thanks.gasp.oven

2. Black Moon Botanica
50 Candlemaker Row; www.
blackmoonbotanica.com
///orange.tent.front

3. Surgeons' Hall Museums
Nicolson Street; www.
museum.rcsed.ac.uk
///shower.runs.fence

4. The Real Mary King's Close
Warriston Close, Royal Mile
www.realmarykingsclose.com
///lungs.rested.hedge;

5. The Witchery by the Castle
352 Castlehill, Royal Mile;
www.thewitchery.com
///clay.grace.slows

The White Hart Inn
///span.wins.events

The White Hart Inn
is the city's oldest pub.
It's where infamous body snatchers Burke and Hare would get their victims drunk.

PRINCES STREET

ESPLANADE

JOHNSTON TERRACE

GRASSMARKET

LAURISTON PLACE

0 metres 150
0 yards 150

WAVERLEY BRIDGE

NORTH BRIDGE

EAST MARKET STREET

**Dare to venture down
THE REAL MARY
KING'S CLOSE**

Explore this eerie warren of
purportedly haunted streets
hidden just beneath the Royal
Mile. Find out about the people
who lived, worked and died here.

HIGH STREET

4 HIGH STREET

HUNTER SQUARE

VNMARKET

PARLIAMENT SQUARE

OLD TOWN

SOUTH BRIDGE

COWGATE

**Stock up on spells at
BLACK MOON
BOTANICA**

An actual candlemaker on
Candlemaker Row? How
fitting. Immerse yourself in
Scotland's pagan roots and
find out your future with a
five-minute tarot reading.

COWGATE

ANDLEMAKER ROW

CHAMBERS STREET

NICOLSON ST

2

1

3

**Explore the graves of
GREYFRIAR'S KIRKYARD**

The names engraved on the tombstones
here are said to have inspired J K Rowling
– look out for a certain Mr Potter, Mrs
McGonagall and the Dark Lord himself,
Thomas Riddell.

SOUTHSIDE

CHAPEL STREET

**See the artifacts at
SURGEONS' HALL
MUSEUMS**

Learn all about gruesome
diseases, dissections and curious
methods of treatment at this
fascinating former anatomy
school-turned-museum.

Edinburgh
University

NIGHTLIFE

Whether it's a spontaneous trad session in a tiny folk pub or a big-name DJ spinning decks in the city's coolest club, options for fun after dark are plentiful.

Live Music

Edinburgh's live music venues have been closing at an alarming rate over the last decade or so, but this vibrant bunch have survived, and they continue to occupy a special place in the hearts of locals.

THE LIQUID ROOM

Map 1; 9C Victoria Street, Old Town; ///oldest.dine.soak; www.liquidroom.com

Both a club and live music venue, indie gem The Liquid Rooms (don't ask us why, the locals will always make it a plural) is the place to check out local talent, big touring bands and some pretty class DJs. Past performers include the likes of Mogwai, Coldplay and the Smashing Pumpkins, to name just a few, and the consistently stellar line-up keeps young alt-rockers and indie kids coming back for more.

STRAMASH

Map 1; 207 Cowgate, Old Town; ///lock.unique.living; www.stramashedinburgh.com

"Stramash" is a Scots word for uproar – pretty fitting for a venue that delivers loud and larger-than-life live performances to an energetic crowd. Apparently 900 gig-goers can fit in this huge converted church but it never feels that way – the space creates a magnetic sense of intimacy despite its size. Expect an eclectic mix of genres, new talent and a seriously sweaty mosh pit.

THE VOODOO ROOMS

Map 3; 19A West Register Street, New Town; ///pretty.cages.tuck; www.thevoodoorooms.com

This lavish cocktail bar and cabaret club is a far cry from your usual Edinburgh gig venue, where empty Red Stripe cans and sweat dripping down the walls are hallmarks of a good night (Liquid Room, we're looking at you). We're talking chandeliers, plush leather seating and opulent décor – a real gilded, gold-studded affair. Here, well-dressed couples cosy up in the shadows of the speakeasy bar and dancers shimmy their way towards the stage in the grand ballroom.

» Don't leave without treating yourself to a cocktail (or two). The bar staff take mixology very seriously; you'll not be disappointed.

THE JAZZ BAR

Map 1; 1A Chambers Street, Old Town; ///gravy.secure.risen; www.thejazzbar.co.uk

Make sure you're in your dancing shoes; things can get pretty wild at Edinburgh's longest-standing independent jazz and funk venue. Incredible local musicians and international guests take to the stage every night, with the energy really ramping up on the weekends. More of a wallflower than a mover and shaker? We've got you. Take a seat at one of the candlelit tables in the corner and enjoy the show.

LEITH DEPOT

**Map 4; 138 Leith Walk, Leith; ///camera.mile.lists;
www.leithdepot.com**

We hate to be the ones to say it, but for a neighbourhood so big on artistic expression, Leith is a wee bit lacking in music venues. One pub changing this is the Leith Depot. This locally loved boozer transforms its upstairs room into a mini gig venue, bringing a genre-spanning spectrum (folk, antifolk, feminist punk) of local bands to its loyal regulars, most of whom the owners know by name.

» Don't leave without having a gander at the food menu – as well as music, Leith Depot is known for serving up some great scran.

HENRY'S CELLAR BAR

**Map 2; 16A Morrison Street, West End; ///lives.launch.spit;
www.henryscellarbar.co.uk**

Ramshackle, unconventional and always a laugh, this tiny basement venue hosts all sorts of class acts, from spoken word to comedy, but it's the promise of loud and live music that really gets punters going.

Try it!
TAKE TO THE STAGE

Henry's Cellar Bar's Easy Mondays Open Stage has been going strong for 15 years. It's a welcoming space for newbies to try out their own material (yup, that's code for no "Wonderwall" covers here, thanks).

Drinks are dirt cheap, as is entry, and the stage is within touching distance of the tiny dance floor, which, by the way, is always total carnage. Sure, you'll probably get beer spilled on you a few times by your fellow dancers as they thrash around to the music but that's all part of the experience, right?

THE QUEEN'S HALL

Map 5; 85–9 Clerk Street, Newington; ///ideal.rival.flag; www.thequeenshall.net

Edinburgh music lovers congregate at this converted Georgian chapel to worship at the feet of rock royalty and give thanks for great tunage. High ceilings and soaring acoustics mean the place is well suited to a variety of performances – of course there's classical (the Queen's Hall is home to the Scottish Chamber Orchestra after all), but the likes of Nina Simone, Nick Cave and Frightened Rabbit have all graced the stage.

BANNERMAN'S

Map 1; 212 Cowgate, Old Town; ///maybe.buns.cling; www.bannermanslive.co.uk

Those looking for a stripped-back session should probably head elsewhere: Bannerman's is all about head-banging hardcore rock, ten-minute guitar solos and Jaegerbombs. Local metal-heads gather in the pub's low-ceilinged front room for a couple of rounds before entering the cavernous back room, where they rock out to their favourite local bands blasting out some serious decibels.

Late-Night Bars

Been kicked out the pub? Not quite ready to hit the club? Edinburgh has loads of late-night bars where locals keep the party going. Pints and pool, sweaty singalongs, sexy speakeasies – which will you choose?

FINGERS PIANO BAR

Map 2; 61A Frederick Street, New Town; ///lost.bath.back; 0131 225 3026

It might be little but this New Town piano bar packs a punch. The drinks are pricey, the crowd is loud and the place is – we'll be honest – pretty sweaty, but there's no better place for a knees-up. Full respect to the pianist who guides the intoxicated crowd through the likes of "Rocketman" and "Sweet Caroline" in the wee hours of the morning.

THE BUNKER

Map 3; 2–6 Calton Road; Old Town ///making.hosts.brass;
www.belhavenpubs.co.uk/pubs/midlothian/bunker

Locals love to hate on the Bunker, but this basement bar is the stuff of legend. It played a starring role in the opening scene of *Trainspotting* (where Renton gives his iconic "Choose Life" speech, remember?), and those out on the razz rely on the cheesy tunes, pool table and cosy corners to keep the party going.

WHISTLE BINKIES

Map 1; 4–6 South Bridge, Old Town; ///august.leader.ropes;
www.whistlebinkies.com

Every Friday and Saturday night rockers congregate for loud, live music at this Edinburgh institution. The floor is sticky and some of the revellers have had one too many but it's all part of the Whistle Binkies experience. The bar also hosts open-mic nights on Mondays.

THE HIGH DIVE

Map 5; 81–5 St Leonard's Street, Southside; ///pills.bring.invent;
www.civerinosthehighdive.com

There's always a hungry crowd waiting outside the High Dive for a slice of restaurateur Michele Civiera's famous pizza. Sound more like NYC than Edinburgh? The Big Apple vibe continues inside, where you'll find a diner with the heart of a dive bar. Office workers choose this chilled-out drinking den for a pick-me-up, pairing pizza with frozen margaritas.

» Don't leave without ordering a Nutella calzone – a fat, folded pizza with banana, raspberry, pistachio and, of course, Nutella. You'll thank us.

THE BANSHEE LABYRINTH

Map 1; 29–35 Niddry Street, Old Town; ///baked.notice.event;
www.thebansheelabyrinth.com

Down in the old vaults, Banshee is said to be the city's most haunted pub, hence its creepy décor. Don't let that put you off: this is a fab spot to catch a band or watch a flick in the bar's tiny cinema. Oh, and good luck finding your pals after a loo break – this place really is a labyrinth.

Solo, Pair, Crowd

Whether you're after a nightcap, a new pal or a midnight feast, Edinburgh's got you covered.

FLYING SOLO

Perch at the bar

Love them or loathe them, Scottish craft beer brewers BrewDog have changed the way we drink beer in the UK. Head to the bar on the Cowgate, where the staff are always happy to talk you through their latest experimental brews.

IN A PAIR

Late-night date night

Hidden beneath Dishoom is the Permit Room, a speakeasy-style bar with a killer cocktail (and mocktail) menu. It's the perfect spot to natter the night away.

FOR A CROWD

Party on with pals

OX184 is loved by locals for offering craft beer by the gallon and some of the best scran you can get in Edinburgh after 1am. It's also wonderfully roomy, so you and your squad can party till the cows come home (it's on the Cowgate, get it?).

NIGHTCAP

Map 3; 3 York Place, New Town; ///case.stale.scales;
www.nightcapbar.co.uk

Keep your eyes peeled for the underground entrance to Nightcap, a cellar-like cocktail bar where the cool kids go to end their night. You could order a classic, but we advise putting your faith in the master mixologists behind the bar to shake you up something special.

» Don't leave without checking out the lineup at The Stand *(p125)* next door, where many of the country's best comedians started.

LADY LIBERTINE

Map 3; 25 West Register Street, St Andrew's Square, New Town;
///finger.giant.bind; www.ladylibertine.co.uk

If you like a bar where you can say "even the toilets are nice", then look no further. Based in the original Royal Bank of Scotland building, Lady Libertine is all about sipping exquisitely crafted cocktails in super-chic surrounds (think marble-top tables, plush seats and moody lighting). Add to that top DJs spinning decks and you've got a sophisticated date spot that's sure to impress.

UNO MASS

Map 3; 4 Picardy Place, Greenside; ///onions.perky.crown;
www.unomasbar.co.uk

Brought to you by music loving, cocktail slinging co-owners Sian Buchan and John Mclellan, Uno Mass is a plush late-night lounge bar hosting live bands and DJs. One more for the road? Oh go on, then.

Cool Clubs

Going out? Or going full on "out out"? Whether you're just donning your trainers or getting properly glammed up, there's one thing you can be sure of: no two Edinburgh nights out are ever the same.

SNEAKY PETE'S

Map 1; 73 Cowgate, Old Town; ///slams.weep.track; www.sneakypetes.co.uk

Open seven nights a week for both club nights and gigs, this minuscule sweatbox is one of the most important nightclubs in Scotland. Owner Nick Stewart is a passionate music venue activist, fighting the good fight to protect the city's independent clubbing scene and live music venues by hosting the city's biggest DJ acts, paving the way for

Shh!

Teviot Underground often gets overlooked because, well, it's underground. But this down-to-earth club is definitely not to be missed. Hidden underneath Edinburgh Uni's famous Library Bar, the venue puts on a class line-up of club nights, great live music gigs and the odd cabaret show to boot. Sure it's all a little bit retro, but that's part of the charm, right?

relative newcomers. Hip hop, techno, house, dub, dancehall and even disco (yup, it's back) all feature. The result? An epic night out in an iconic Edinburgh venue that will not be forgotten.

» **Don't leave without** checking out Sneaky Pete's merch behind the bar to get your hands on the coolest T-shirts and tote bags in town.

THE BONGO CLUB

Map 1; 66 Cowgate, Old Town; ///this.precautions.steps; www.thebongoclub.co.uk

On Tuesday nights an energetic young crowd seeking more than just chart hits gets in line at the Bongo Club for I Love Hip Hop. Expect all the classics, plus a generous helping of the best new MCs on the scene. In need of a wee breather? The garden area out back is the place to chat, flirt and make new pals – that is until the next banger comes on and the crowd makes its way back to the dance floor.

THE MASH HOUSE

Map 1; 37 Guthrie Street, Old Town; ///shunts.free.shuts; www.themashhouse.co.uk

Ah, the Mash House. This place has changed hands so many times over the years it's hard to keep track, but with each iteration the club lodges itself deeper in the hearts of locals. Looking for lively club nights and some good old multi-genre experimentation? Across TMH's three floors you'll hear thumping house, techno and drum and base spun by resident DJs, plus some funk, soul and reggae thrown in for good measure.

CABARET VOLTAIRE

Map 1; 36 Blair Street, Old Town; ///poems.harsh.fines;
www.thecabaretvoltaire.com

Most Edinburgh locals have spent one too many a Friday night (and Saturday morning) dancing their socks off to house or techno in Cab Vol's cavernous underground vaults. This sweaty dance fest is where local resident DJs are revered like kings by the adoring crowd. The music is loud, the crowd is wild and the energy is infectious.

LA BELLE ANGELE

Map 1; 11 Hasties Close, Old Town; ///maybe.buns.cling;
www.la-belleangele.com

Having hosted the likes of Oasis, the Libertines and Shooglenifty, this place was one of the city's most important music venues before it was destroyed in a fire in 2002. But, like a phoenix rising from the ashes, La Belle is back and it's bigger and better than ever. Expect a solid number of club nights in its 600-capacity space, international DJs like Nic Fanciulli and Hunee spinning the decks, and esteemed guests like DJ Craig Charles with his legendary Funk and Soul Club.

THE WEE RED BAR

Map 2; 74 Lauriston Place, Lauriston; ///spoken.liner.vibes;
www.weeredbar.co.uk

Edinburgh College of Art's adorable little venue and club is always packed. And, before you say it, this place isn't your usual student dive, thanks to a constant line-up of great gigs and club nights. The music is varied (think reggae to post-rock), drinks are cheap (surprisingly so) and the vibe is super casual, which always makes for a fun night out (it's always a bonus when you can dance the night away in your trainers). Regular club nights include Hey QT (an uber-fabulous gay glitter disco) and The Egg, a smorgasbord of soul and disco that's been going since time immemorial, or so it seems.

» Don't leave without checking out the Art College's sculpture hall, though maybe best to come back at a more godly hour?

LULU

Map 2; 125 George Street, New Town;
///voices.charge.hints; www.tigerlilyedinburgh.co.uk

Lulu is where the stylish masses head when they're in the mood for a proper fancy night out. It's pricey and, yes, a bit performative, but you get what you pay for: private booths, a VIP area and a *Saturday Night Fever*-style light-up dance floor that proves nobody's too posh to get down and boogie to the latest chart, house and R 'n' B hits.

EL BARRIO

Map 2; 119 Rose Street, New Town; ///tummy.powder.bonus;
www.elbarrio.com

Tequila, salsa and "Despacito" played on repeat: it's a combination that, if you're in the right mood, makes El Barrio stupid amounts of fun. This Latin American basement bar and club is all about winding hips and feel-good tunes. Take salsa lessons here at the weekends, and then hit the club at night to show off your moves.

LGBTQ+ Scene

Gay, bi, queer, allies – everyone's welcomed with open arms here in Edinburgh's Pink Triangle, where the city's most inclusive lounge bars and clubs promise a truly fabulous night out.

THE STREET

Map 3; 2b Picardy Place, New Town; ///tiles.herds.simple; www.thestreetbaredinburgh.co.uk

Welcome to the Burgh's youngest gay bar, where a buzzy atmosphere and bargain pints have earned it an enduring popularity with an equally young crowd. If lively bops and classic cocktails are what get you in the mood to party, you can do a lot worse than The Street.

PARADISE PALMS

Map 1; Lothian Street, Southside; ///shells.trade.analogy; www.theparadisepalms.com

Pinning Palms down under one banner is tricky – and that's exactly why it's so special. This rainbow-flag-flying tropical-themed bar, club, restaurant, record label, shop and festival venue (phew, we got there in the end) is where the coolest kids in the city hang out. Inclusivity and creativity are the order of the day, and local DJs, musicians and

Post Palms head next door to Boteco for Latin tunes, frozen margaritas and a lively dance floor. | artists from all walks of life are all part of the Palms community. Weekends get wild with cabaret and drag performances from big names on the local circuit.

PLANET BAR & KITCHEN

Map 3; 6 Baxter's Place, Greenside; ///unique.strain.sang; www.planetbaredinburgh.co.uk

Strong roots in the community make Edinburgh's longest running gay bar a focal point of warmth in the city's gay scene, and it shows – the staff are friendly, the queens are sassy and the crowd all seem to know each other. Sing your heart out at Planet's riotous karaoke nights (Tuesdays, Thursdays and Sundays) – just be prepared to have a drag queen decimate your performance before your final note has rung out.

THE REGENT

Map 3; 2 Montrose Terrace, Abbeyhill; ///along.zone.string; www.theregentbar.co.uk

Looking for something a bit more chilled? The Regent is the best spot to while away a Sunday afternoon lounging on a chesterfield sofa, petting a stranger's dog with one hand and nursing a pint in the other. Peruse a varied pub grub menu as you laugh with your mates over the antics of the night before. And who knows, when the pub closes at 1am, you might just be tempted to hit the town. Or not. You do you.

» Don't leave without trying a pint of Bellfield Brewery's gluten-free Lawless IPA. It's made just down the road from the Regent.

CC BLOOMS

Map 3; 23–4 Greenside Place, Greenside; ///visual.lungs.park;
www.ccblooms.co.uk

Here you have it. The beating, vodka-soaked heart of gay Edinburgh.
This place has a reputation among local twinks as the place to see
and be seen, and boy do they know how to belt out a cheese and
charts pop singalong that lasts well into the wee hours. Sure, drinks
might be a touch on the spenny side, but with two busy bars split
across two dance floors and no let up until 3am (or 5am during the
Edinburgh Festival in August) there's a reason that CC's is where the
party always ends up. Every Tuesday night regulars head downstairs
to see the very best of local drag in The Rabbit Hole, hosted by the
fabulous Alice Rabbit herself, of course.

» Don't leave without letting your hair down on the dance floor in
CC's basement club, where everything is that bit louder and wilder.

CAFÉ HABANA

Map 3; 22 Greenside Place, Greenside; ///matter.watch.social;
0131 558 1270

Just next door to CC's is Café Habana. It may be the smaller
of the pair, but it still packs a solid punch, and punters of all
persuasions parade around the central dance floor like nobody's
business. This compact space attracts all sorts – gay, non-gay,
young and let's just say the young at heart (ahem). Need a bit of
a breather? Grab some drinks from the bar and guide them up
the spiral staircase to the chilled-out seating area. Your calves
will thank you for taking a wee break from all that dancing.

Liked by the locals

It may be small, but Edinburgh's gay scene is a close-knit community that boasts big nights and great drag acts in the eclectic venues of the city's famous "Pink Triangle".

RYAN MATTHEWSON,
COMEDIAN, CAT DAD AND LGBTQ+ EVENT HOST

Games Night

Fun is the name of the game in the Burgh. Of course locals love to sit in a pub and shoot the breeze, but a pub fitted out with pinball machines, board games and ping pong tables? Now we're talking.

4042

Map 2; 40–42 Grindlay Street, Tollcross; ///noisy.mice.both; www.4042.co.uk

Can't decide between clubbing and a bit of healthy competition? Thankfully, 4042 does both. Park yourself at the ping pong hall at the back of this late night bar, where paddles arrive in champagne buckets, cocktails come adorned with candy and hip hop beats have you bouncing off the walls until 3am. Ping pong not your thing? There are pop-up quizzes, karaoke and cinema nights here too.

MOUSETRAP

Map 4; 180 Leith Walk, Leith; ///outer.flame.hurls; 0131 553 0220

Spot the retro game and Rubik's cube graffiti on the outside of this dive bar and you'll know you're in the right place. Pinball wizards and Pac-Man pros bypass the bar area and make a beeline for the back room, where they fight for the highest scores in this 80s-style arcade. Thankfully cheap-as-chips cocktails and cheese toasties provide an extra life to those looking for sustenance IRL.

» Don't leave without spinning the wheel behind the bar to let fate decide what drink you'll go for next.

THE SHEEP HEID INN
Map 6; 43–5 The Causeway, Duddingston; ///create.photos.tell; www.thesheepheidedinburgh.co.uk

Muddy-booted locals tucking into hearty dinners while their dogs snooze happily by the crackling open hearth – this place is everything a country pub should be. But wait, there's more. The wooden-beamed room out back, affectionately dubbed Skittle Alley, is where you and your mates can play against each other in the game rumoured to have been a favourite of King James and Mary Queen of Scots – they're even said to have played it on this very site, way back in the day. A word to the wise: be sure to book in advance. This spot has been popular for centuries after all.

Try it!
GET QUIZZICAL

Check Pub Quizzy *(www.pubquizzy.com)* for a list of pub quizzes in the city, organized by day of the week. If you ask us, the best of the lot is Monday night at the Pear Tree *(p68)* with quiz master Dave.

FORE PLAY CRAZY GOLF

Map 3; 14 Picardy Place, New Town; ///crew.sheep.tribes;
www.foreplaycrazygolf.co.uk

Nine wacky holes make up this innuendo-infused pop-up golf course
cheekily named "Wee Bobby" (a name that elicits at least a chuckle
from locals in the know). Rub Bobby's nose for good luck, and guide
your balls through loop the loops, ramps and a grand finale on a mini
Scott Monument. After your game, step right up for some tasty street
food and golf-themed cocktails, like May the Course be With You or
Does my Putt Look Big in This?

NQ64 ARCADE BAR

Map 2; 25 Lothian Road, West End; ///comic.calls.secure;
www.nq64.co.uk

Packed out with retro consoles and arcade games, and set to the
soundtrack of concentrated thumb tapping, this is where the Burgh's
hipsters come for a bit of gaming nostalgia. Evenings are frittered
away going square-eyed on Pac-Man or battling it out in an intense
gaming tournament. Whoever loses buys the next round.

SUPERCUBE

Map 4; 58A George Street, New Town; ///plus.rotate.soup;
www.supercube.biz

Edinburgh locals love a sing-song; whether they can actually sing
is another question entirely. Thankfully Supercube's Japanese-style
private karaoke rooms mean gaggles of pals, talented or tone deaf,

Book a room in advance to get bonus time, pizza packages and some bargain midweek deals.

can clamber all over the sofas and sing their wee hearts out in the most imperfect way without the embarrassment of an entire bar listening in.

WINGS

Map 1; 5–7 Old Fishmarket Close, Old Town; ///herds.twist.alone; www.sauceedinburgh.com

Not only does this place serve up the best fried chicken in the city (a bold claim, but one we stand by), it's also a hub for local gamers looking to get in on some multiplayer action. GameCube, X-Box or Nintendo 64 are just some of the retro consoles to choose from.

» Don't leave without buying a bottle of Wings' secret sauce. Hot, fruity, BBQ, you got it – all with fun, comic book-style labels.

DEPARTMENT OF MAGIC: PROPHECIES QUEST

Map 1; 9 Blair Street, Old Town; ///ranges.actors.fend; www.departmentofmagic.com

Don your wizard robes (provided by the premises), and make the age-old decision: good or evil? Through elaborate storytelling, detailed set design and riddles fit for the cleverest of witches, this place will transport you to the magical realm. Even if you don't play the full escape quest, pull up a stool at the Potions Tavern, make your own cocktail concoctions or, in the afternoon, spot students doing what we can only assume is Transfiguration homework.

Scottish Evenings and Session Bars

While Edinburgh is in many ways a modern city, Scottish tradition still plays a big part in daily life. Locals listen in on impromptu folk sessions in cosy pubs and ceilidh the night away until the wee hours.

CAPTAIN'S BAR

Map 1; 4 South College Street, Southside; ///times.online.pound; www.captainsedinburgh.webs.com

A fierce advocate for Scottish trad, Captain's big-hearted landlady Pam puts on quite the show. Informal folk sessions and acoustic acts perform nightly in her nautical-themed pub, where instruments line the walls and a sea captain's ghost resides behind the bar (apparently).

GHILLIE DHU

Map 2; 2 Rutland Place, West End; ///dined.riots.dozed; www.ghillie-dhu.co.uk

Ye dancin'? Ye askin'? A far cry from forced social dances of school days gone by, Ghillie Dhu is where locals looking for a bit of Scottish flair get their ceilidh on, and boy do they gie it laldy. While the pub itself is nothing special, the opulent auditorium, with its high-vaulted ceilings, candlelit chandeliers and tartan everywhere, is where the magic really happens. Enjoy dinner and a dance with the Rabbie Burns Supper Club, or show up after 9pm for the ceilidh and live band. And don't worry, learning the steps as you go is half the fun.

THE BLACK CAT

Map 2; 168 Rose Street, New Town; ///lunch.desk.clouds;
www.theblackcatbar.com

Rightly considered too cramped for Rose Street's usual rabble of drunken stag dos (thank goodness for that), The Black Cat has garnered a small but loyal crowd of discerning regulars. Sure, they come here primarily for the rare whiskies and impressive craft beer selection (one of the finest in the country) but they end up staying for the live folk music, merrily tapping along in time as they sip their drinks and chatter between tunes.

» Don't leave without tucking into some top-notch nibbles while you're here. Think Scotch pies and haggis bon bons with a whisky sauce.

Try it!
JOIN IN WITH A JIG

Most Edinburgh session pubs encourage audience participation, so if you play an instrument, bring it along and join right in. Didn't bring your fiddle? Don't let that stop you – there's usually one kicking around.

Liked by the locals

"Edinburgh has a trad music session for every day of the week, with a tremendous variety of styles on offer. My go-tos are Sandy Bell's, Captain's Bar, The Black Cat and ending the night at The Royal Oak – if you can make it to 2am."

LUISA BROWN,
MUSICIAN AND FOLK SESSION FIDDLER

THE ROYAL OAK

Map 1; 1 Infirmary Street, Southside; ///listed.kinds.covers;
www.royal-oak-folk.com

A stalwart among the city's session bars, The Royal Oak has hosted
some big names on the Scottish music scene. On Sunday nights join
folk-loving locals as they grab a pint from the bar and head downstairs
to the Wee Folk Club to discover a new-found love for Scottish trad.

LEITH FOLK CLUB

Map 6; 221 Ferry Road, Leith; ///silent.glitz.prefer;
www.leithfolkclub.com

Taking over the function room in the Victoria Park House Hotel every
Tuesday, this community folk club is a hoot and a half. Aye, there are
the usual fiddle bands you'd expect to see, but this is no place for
purists: think contemporary folk, Americana and even a bit of country.

SANDY BELL'S

Map 1; 25 Forrest Road, Old Town; ///become.term.reward;
www.sandybells.com

Entering this tiny old-school boozer is like stumbling in on a private
rehearsal: huddled at the back, the band don't intend to entertain,
they're just playing for the love for it. A toe-tapping audience munching
on bags of crisps to upbeat jigs is simply a bonus. It may be small, but
this wee place is a huge name on the international trad circuit.

» Don't leave without having a friendly chat with whoever's playing
that night – they're here for a good time too, after all.

Princes
Street
Gardens

MARKET STREET

NORTH BANK ST

HIGH STREE

Line your stomach at
HANAM'S

Sit outside overlooking
the seriously picturesque
Victoria Street (every
local's favourite street in
Edinburgh) and enjoy
shisha and Middle
Eastern sharing platters
with your pals.

LAWNMARKET

OLD TOWN

Catch a gig at
SNEAKY PETE'S

The capacity might only
be 100 people but this
iconic live music venue
and clubbing spot is
easily one of the best
nights out in the city.

COWGATE

2

WEST BOW

TERRACE

JOHNSTON

4

CANDLEMAKER ROW

GRASSMARKET

3

In 1724 "Half-Hangit
Maggie" was hanged,
only to come back to life
the next day. The pub
Maggie Dickson's is
named after her.

Have a cocktail at
UNDER THE STAIRS

Sip on creative cocktails
with a seasonal focus at
this sophisticated Old Town
basement bar, where the
vibe is cosy, casual and
candlelit. Cheers.

1

Enjoy a sundowner at
COLD TOWN
HOUSE

Grab a pre-dinner beer
at this microbrewery in
an enormous renovated
church. Drink it all in with
spectacular castle views
from the rooftop terrace.

FORREST ROAD

TEVIOT PLACE

LAURISTON PLACE

0 metres	125
0 yards	125

A night out in the
Old Town

Beneath the polished streets of George IV Bridge is the Cowgate, Edinburgh's dark and dingy under-belly, lined with dive bars, live music venues and some of the best clubs in the city. For centuries this is where the bulk of Edinburgh's debauchery has taken place. The name dates back to the 1490s, when farmers brought livestock along the then-called Via Vaccarum ("way of the cows") to the city's cattle market, which was kept as far away as possible from the eyes (and delicate noses) of Edinburgh's high society.

5

Afterparty at OX184

Not ready to go home? Head to late-night favourite OX184 for a nightcap by the open fire. What's more, it runs a full food menu until late, ideal if you're feeling peckish.

1. Cold Town House
4 Grassmarket; www.
coldtown house.co.uk
///buzz.oppose.parks

2. Hanam's
3 Johnson Terrace;
www.hanams.com
///shave.than.camera

3. Under the Stairs
3A Merchant Street;
www.underthestairs.org
///cube.locked.friday

4. Sneaky Pete's
73 Cowgate; www.
sneakypetes.co.uk
///slams.weep.track

5. OX184
184–6 Cowgate;
www.ox184.co.uk
///boring.expect.lake

Maggie Dickson's
///traps.ideas.remind

OUTDOORS

Locals here have an insatiable appetite for the great outdoors. Fortunately, rugged mountains, sandy beaches and sprawling parks are all part and parcel of city life.

Green Spaces

Edinburgh's green spaces are a huge part of local life: they're the setting for picnics on those fleeting sunny days and drizzly walks when it's dreich. Whatever the weather, there's a park beckoning.

PRINCES STREET GARDENS

Map 2; entrance via Princes Street, New Town; ///liner.ending.tens

Nestled between the new and old towns, this tree-dotted grassy garden offers the perfect slice of calm and quiet from nearby Princes Street, with its crowds of jostling tourists and eager-eyed shoppers. Stop to take a pew on one of the park's benches, listen to the sound of the fountain and gaze up at the castle, which sits serenely above.

» Don't leave without finding the floral cuckoo clock. First planted in 1903, the design is updated with a fresh arrangement each year.

THE MEADOWS

Map 5; entrance via Melville Drive, Southside; ///gold.bags.steep; www.themeadowsofedinburgh.co.uk

Essentially the city's back garden, this sprawling park is found a hop, skip and a jump away from Edinburgh University's main campus area. Students spread out on the grass for a sunny study sesh or undertake the more serious job of playing Quidditch (keep your eyes peeled for the person dressed as the snitch). But this place isn't just for students: Edinburgh locals flock to this beloved green space to stroll beneath the cherry trees, potter in the cute community garden or enjoy a few tinnies in the sun with friends.

ROYAL BOTANIC GARDEN

Map 6; entrance via Arboretum Place, Inverleith;
///making.maps.navy; www.rbge.org.uk

Yes, these gardens are a famed scientific research centre, but they're also simply a beautiful place to get lost in nature. Young families and meandering couples certainly think so, indulging their botanical curiosity in the woodland glade and intricate rock garden here. Entry to the glasshouses – complete with giant waterlilies and more cacti than you can shake a stick at – is ticketed, but you can wander the rest of the gardens for free (or donate; it helps the plants thrive).

INVERLEITH PARK

Map 6; entrance via East Fettes Avenue, Inverleith;
///liked.fades.trying; www.friendsofinverleithpark.co.uk

Families rule this roost during the week, feeding the ducks at the pretty pond. But on a weekend you'll find amateur teams making use of the playing fields, dogs a-scampering and market-goers spilling onto the picnic lawns with their takeaway hauls. One bench in particular, just up from the pond, is the perfect spot to catch the sunset over the city (the w3w address is: ///piano.junior.they. You're welcome).

ARTHUR'S SEAT AND HOLYROOD PARK

Map 6; entrance via Queen's Drive, Holyrood; ///rocket.tend.caller;
www.historicenvironment.scot/visit-a-place/places/holyrood-park

Where else can you find towering cliffs, an extinct volcano and
tranquil lochs right in the middle of a city? Nowhere but the Burgh's
Holyrood Park, that's where. In this wild spot you can spy otters and
swans at tiny Dunsapie Loch, take a stroll beneath the imposing
rock face of the Salisbury Crags and then huff and puff your way
to the top of the once-fiery volcano Arthur's Seat for panoramic
360-degree views across the whole city.

DR NEIL'S GARDEN

Map 6; entrance via 15 Old Church Lane, Duddingston;
///grow.softly.theme; www.drneilsgarden.co.uk

Lying in the shadow of Arthur's Seat, the city's very own "secret
garden" was set up by doctors Nancy and Andrew Neil in the
1960s. The husband-and-wife team filled this little loch-side oasis

Just off the Royal Mile is
Dunbar's Close, a hidden
17th-century-style walled
garden that feels like you've
stumbled into a laird's fancy,
surprisingly floral courtyard.

Even though it's open to the
public, genuinely not many
people know about it, making it
the perfect spot to escape the
Old Town's bustle if you need to
check out for a minute or two.

with plants and young trees – sourced from their caravan travels round Europe – and prescribed gardening at this restorative spot to their patients. Today, the garden is still volunteer-run and a favourite place for those seeking a wee bit of solitude.

>> Don't leave without having a coffee and slice of cake at the peaceful on-site Garden Room Café, also run by local volunteers.

GEORGE SQUARE GARDENS

Map 5; entrance via George Square, Southside; ///media.bucket.magic

Surrounded by university buildings, this leafy sanctuary, complete with its own circular labyrinth, is where essay-hounded students come to escape the stresses of academia. You won't recognize it during the summer though. When festival season is in full swing, this place transforms into a chaotic maze of pop-up bars, sizzling street food stalls and elaborately decorated stages that host some of the top acts of the Edinburgh Jazz and Blues, Fringe and international festivals.

CRAIGMILLAR CASTLE PARK

Map 6; entrance via Old Dalkeith Road, Craigmillar;
///prompting.rooms.secure; 0131 529 2401

After a taste of rural Scotland? Try Craigmillar Castle Park. It might be within the city, but this natural heritage spot feels like a slice of countryside thanks to its flower-dotted fields and numerous leafy trees (40,000 were planted here in 1997 as part of the Millennium Forest for Scotland project). Oh, and you'll also find the city's second castle, a 15th-century ruin that once played host to Mary Queen of Scots.

Scenic Strolls

The twists and turns of Edinburgh's many walking routes enchant and confuse even the locals. But don't let that put you off. Forget your itinerary and explore this city's waterside paths and historic streets.

UNION CANAL

Map 5; start at Lochrin Basin, Fountainbridge; ///vocal.bets.cheek

Come rain or shine, fitness-obsessed joggers, walkers and cyclists can be found along the leafy paths that line this scenic stretch of water. Sure, you could try and impress them by taking on the whole shebang – the Union Canal runs all the way to rival city Glasgow some 50 km (30 miles) away – but we recommend taking on the short section from Lochrin Basin, the canal's city-centre start point, to Colinton. Perfect for a serene afternoon stroll by the water.

HERMITAGE OF BRAID

Map 5; start at 69 Hermitage of Braid, Blackford; ///sadly.direct.smashes

Nestled between the Braid Hills and Blackford Hill, this ancient woodland makes for a great stroll. Visit on sunny weekends and you'll see crowds of families, lolloping dogs in tow, meandering along the paths that weave beneath the trees. Fancy a river walk? Follow the

 Want to do your bit? Community group Friends of the Braid Hills runs clean-ups and volunteer sessions.

path that runs alongside Blackford River (a favourite swimming spot for dogs). After a bit of peace and quiet? The lesser known Braid Bridle Path will do the trick.

ROYAL MILE

**Map 1; start near the Gatehouse of Edinburgh Castle,
Old Town; ///frosted.chart.eggs**

This iconic mile-long medieval walk stretches from Edinburgh Castle to the Palace of Holyroodhouse (summer hangout of Queen Lizzy). Scurry past the souvenir shops swathed in tartan and blasting bagpipe music; the real magic of this cobblestone street is found when you dip down the dark wynds and secret closes that branch off the Mile. Even better: some lead to hidden courtyards, such as Lady Stair's Close, a narrow wee alley that opens out into Makar's Court, whose flagstones are inscribed with the words of famous Scottish writers.

» Don't leave without nipping inside St Giles Cathedral for a peek at the ornate interior, especially the colour-popping stained glass.

Try it!
GO ORIENTEERING

The Braid Hills are home to a permanent orienteering course with 21 control points (*www.goorienteering.org.uk*). It's pretty contained, so even if a sense of direction isn't your strong point, you can't get too lost.

DEAN VILLAGE

**Map 2; start at the junction of Kerr and Saunders streets,
Stockbridge; ///flags.shot.lamp**

The 38-km- (24-mile-) long Water of Leith Walkway wiggles its
way through central Edinburgh using a network of disused railway
paths. Our favourite patch? The beautifully lush section that runs
from Stockbridge to the seriously picturesque Dean Village, engulfing
walkers in a dreamy, secluded grove complete with a deep river
gorge and Roman temple-style monuments. Lovely stuff.

CALTON HILL

Map 3; start on Regent Road, New Town; ///races.nets.fear

Calton Hill might be famed for its mishmash of historic monuments,
including the telescope-esque Nelson Monument and Pantheon-
inspired National Monument, but this isn't why locals come here.
No, they come for the cracking views across the city. In fact, you
know that quintessential shot of Edinburgh? The one looking over

Shh!

Most locals stroll unknowingly
past St Bernard's Well, a Greco-
Roman-style temple overlooking
the Water of Leith. Little do they
know that its old pump house
contains a bejewelled interior,
including a deep-blue tiled
ceiling decorated with teeny-
tiny mosaic stars that glitter in
the light and a radiant golden
sun. This has to be the prettiest
pump house you ever did see.

the castle, Old Town and Scott Monument? That's taken from just behind the hill's Greek-inspired Dugald Stewart Monument. Make your way to the top for sunset and get ready to gawp.

» **Don't leave without** spending an hour or two gazing at the contemporary visual art in the Collective gallery *(p131)*, found inside the hill's old city observatory.

COLINTON DELL

Map 6; start at Water of Leith Visitor Centre, 24 Lanark Road, Colinton; ///trying.strong.dose

The beautifully wooded area of Colinton Dell is just under 8 km (5 miles) from the city centre, so you won't have to go far to get lost in the trees. In summer, the forest paths are heady with the smell of wild garlic and blackberries, and whatever the season, you'll be treated to views of the thundering weir. Look out too for the kaleido-scopic designs by muralist Chris Rutterford that line the inside of the old Victorian railway tunnel.

CORSTORPHINE HILL

Map 6; start on Corstorphine Road, Corstorphine; ///soaks.from.joined

Edinburgh is known for its seven hills and this is one of them. Leafy Corstorphine offers a great lookout across the city, plus stunning views over the Firth of Forth to the north. Amble along its crisscrossing wooded paths, favoured by dog walkers and their energetic pups, and keep an eye out for the little-known Walled Garden; this pretty spot is well-cared for by local green-fingered volunteers.

By the Sea

Edinburgh's seaside location is often overlooked. But the sea is a huge draw for locals, who love nothing more than walking against the salty sea breeze or feasting on the catch of the day.

PORTOBELLO

Map 6; Promenade, Portobello; ///marble.jazz.fumes; www.porty.org.uk

Ah Porty, you beauty. Edinburgh's closest seaside neighbourhood is dearly loved by locals; after all, it's where most of them come to get a taste of sea, sand and – if they're very, very lucky – sun. This weathered and well-trodden spot is a quirky mix of old-school businesses (including a retro arcade, which comes complete with the usual garish fluorescent lighting) and new hipster spots (who

Try it!
ON THE WATER

Salty sea dogs head straight for Port Edgar Watersports CIC *(www.portedgar.co.uk/ watersports)*. One of the largest water sports centres in Scotland, it offers courses in dinghy sailing, sea kayaking, SUP and more.

doesn't love an effortlessly cool bakery or bagel shop?). Wander along the endless prom with the dog walkers and beach runners, keeping an eye out for the fearless wild swimmers who throw themselves into the sea come rain or shine, wind or snow.

THE SHORE

Map 4; The Shore, Leith; ///trades.drove.ahead

Found near the point where every Edinburger's favourite river (the Water of Leith, of course) meets the Firth, this pretty riverside spot is the heart of the Leith neighbourhood. Once a working industrial port, The Shore is today a bougie area: think cute cobblestone streets lined with wine cafés, top-class fish restaurants, old-school pubs and quirky local shops selling everything from candles to craft beer.

» Don't leave without popping into the Malt & Hops, a pint-sized pub offering real ales and (for those winter days) a roaring fire.

NEWHAVEN HARBOUR

Map 6; Pier Place, Newhaven; ///civil.grain.curvy

There's one big reason to head to Newhaven Harbour: the seafood. This oceanside spot is, after all, where local fisherfolk bring in their day's catch, fresh from the icy waters of the North Sea. So it's no surprise that the area is awash (ahem) with places to chow down on ocean scran. Spy locals picking up fresh fish from family-run Welch Fishmongers and then head to the Fishmarket to grab a sizzling fish supper, complete with chips doused liberally in Edinburgh's secret-recipe salt 'n' sauce (no vinegar here, thanks).

SOUTH QUEENSFERRY

**Map 6; South Queensferry Harbour, South Queensferry;
///competing.jungle.outlast; www.theforthbridges.org**

If you're after a place to boggle at Edinburgh's famous bridges, look
no further than South Queensferry. Nestled on the edge of the Firth
of Forth, this bonnie town rustles up uninterrupted views over all
three bridges that span its inky waters, including the iconic iron
arches of the rust-red Forth Rail Bridge. Even better, you're guaranteed
to spot Kevin Bridges; no, we don't mean the famous Scottish
comedian, but the newly built Queensferry Crossing road bridge,
so-named by comedy-loving locals. Beyond the bridges, the town
itself is definitely worth a wee neb, thanks to its seaside pubs and
restaurants, indie boutiques and seriously cute cafés.

» Don't leave without checking out the displays in the Queensferry
Museum about how the Forth Rail Bridge was built.

CRAMOND

**Map 6; free parking at Glebe Road, Cramond;
///rates.curiosity.wires; www.cramondassociation.org.uk**

With its cute-as-a-button whitewashed cottages, sandy beach and
harbour dotted with fishing boats, Cramond can't help but exude
postcard vibes. And would you have it, this pretty village is the oldest
known site of human settlement in all of Scotland, having been a
Roman fort and a medieval parish in days gone by. Nowadays it's a
regular seaside getaway for Edinburgers wanting to blow away the
cobwebs, venturing out along a stony causeway to the uninhabited
Cramond Island when the tide is low. On their return they'll pop in

Check the tide times if going to Cramond Island; unprepared walkers have been stranded there before.

to the Cramond Inn for a pint and a plate of chips. Fancy an even longer wander? Follow the picturesque River Almond upstream from the beach.

EAST LOTHIAN COAST

Map 6; East Lothian; www.visiteastlothian.org

Okay, yes – there are plenty of pretty seaside spots a stone's throw from the capital. But if you want a more secluded option, try going a wee bit further afield to the East Lothian Coast, a stunning stretch of coastline peppered with sea-whipped stony bays and rugged sandy beaches. Local faves include Gullane, a blink-and-you'll-miss-it town with a horseshoe sandy cove, and Seacliff, a curved beach with views of the ruined Tantallon Castle. And when you're tired of the Burgh's windy, dreich weather? Dunbar will cheer you up. This historic town is known for its high sunshine record – although, since this is Scotland, maybe that's not saying much. Ah well, there's always the castle, rugged coastline and nearby beach to explore.

Venture even further along the coast and you'll reach St Abb's Head. Not far from the border with England, this coastal nature reserve is known for its rugged cliffs and is home to thousands of seabirds. Visit in summer when the birds are nesting and wildflowers such as wild thyme blanket the cliff tops.

Outdoor Adventures

Despite the usual stereotypes, Edinburgers are a pretty sporty bunch. Whether cycling, skiing or braving the chilly waters of the North Sea, locals love to don their activewear and work up a sweat.

WILD SWIMMING AT WARDIE BAY

Map 6; start from the Eastern Breakwater just off Lower Granton Road, Granton; ///pipes.lowest.palm

Fancy taking the plunge into Scotland's famously chilly waters? Try Wardie Bay. It might not be as picturesque as Portobello to the east, but this tiny sand-and-stone beach has its own rugged charm, plus it's much less much crowded. Plan a dip for a Sunday afternoon and you'll get to meet the Wardie Bay Wild Ones, a group of hardy (or foolhardy?) locals who regularly brave the waves. We salute you all.

AKWAKATING ON THE UNION CANAL

Map 6; start from the Bridge 8 Hub on Calder Crescent, Wester Hailes; ///lived.stacks.stops; 07808 534028

Once used to bring coal from Glasgow to Edinburgh, Union Canal is now dotted with a flotilla of rowers, kayakers and paddle boarders. You could join them, or you could go akwakating. Offered by the folks at Bridge 8 Hub, this unusual (some might say bizarre) activity involves pedalling across the water on what can only be described as a bike-boat. Well, at least you won't blend in with the crowd.

CYCLE ON THE JOHN MUIR WAY

**Map 6; start next to the Forth Railbridge Viewpoint, Newhalls Road,
South Queensferry; ///divisible.youth.hoops; www.johnmuirway.org**
You might think Edinburgh, with all of its many, many hills, isn't the best spot to adventure on two wheels. But you'd be wrong. In fact, a section of the John Muir Way – a 215-km (134-mile) long-distance trail that extends all the way from Helensburgh on the west coast of Scotland to Dunbar on the east – runs right through the city. Most folk tackle a small section in a day, but the really hardcore will make a trip of it, strapping bags of kit to their trusty steeds and setting off for a multi-day bikepacking adventure.

HIT THE SLOPES AT MIDLOTHIAN SNOWSPORTS CENTRE

Map 6; Biggar Road, Midlothian; ///spared.wires.puns; 0131 445 4433
Okay, it's hardly on a par with the powdery slopes of the French Alps, but this city is home to the largest artificial ski slope in the UK. Locally known as Hillend, this centre in the Pentlands is where snow-obsessed ski bums learnt the basics – complete with a few gnarly crashes into the air bags at the foot of the slopes.
» Don't leave without taking the half-hour hike up Caerketton, the 488-m (1,601-ft) peak behind Hillend, for panoramic views over the city.

Solo, Pair, Crowd

Whether you're chasing a new PB or you prefer to spectate from the terraces, Edinburgh's got you covered.

FLYING SOLO
Take a hike
The rolling hills of the Pentlands on the outskirts of Edinburgh are a hiker's dream. Climb Allermuir for beautiful views over Edinburgh, Fife and the Lammermuir Hills, or head to Harlaw, Glencorse or Bonaly Reservoir for a seriously scenic day out.

IN A PAIR
Rackets at the ready
Grab a pal and make for the Meadows, Edinburgh's most famous park, for a game of tennis. You'll find 16 outdoor tennis courts here, as well as the Andy Murray mural on the clubhouse nearby.

IN A CROWD
Catch a match
Visiting with a gaggle of mates? Head to one of the city's stadiums to watch Hearts or Hibs – the city's rival footy teams – play a fast-paced game. The former play at Tynecastle Park, the latter at Easter Road.

PITCH AND PUTT AT BRUNTSFIELD LINKS

**Map 5; start at the Golf Tavern, Bruntsfield Links, Bruntsfield;
///normal.piper.behave; www.bruntsfieldshortholegolfclub.co.uk**

Scotland is the birthplace of golf, so it's no wonder that the area around Edinburgh is awash with courses (just under 70, in fact). Right in the heart of the city is Bruntsfield Links, home to a casual-as-it-gets 36-hole pitch-and-putt course. Hire clubs and balls from the historic Golf Tavern, found on the western edge of the Links, and get swinging. Surprisingly few of the balls manage to find their way onto the main roads nearby – something the neighbours are eternally grateful for.

» Don't leave without nipping into the almost 600-year-old Golf Tavern for hearty post-play pub grub and a pint of craft beer.

STARGAZING AT BLACKFORD HILL

**Map 5; start at the Royal Observatory of Scotland, Blackford Hill,
Blackford; ///laptop.wiped.prompting; www.roe.ac.uk**

Best known for its epic views of the Pentland Hills, the castle and Arthur's Seat, Blackford Hill – one of the Burgh's famous seven summits – is also the perfect spot to stargaze. After all, it's been home to the Royal Observatory of Scotland since 1786. Head to one of the observatory's public open evenings to peek at the night sky through its powerful telescope, or simply wrap up warm (even if it's summer), find a spot outside and gaze skywards. Fair warning: the clouds have been known to sit stubbornly overhead on occasion, but don't worry – the views over the twinkling city skyline will more than make up for any lack of stellar display above.

Nearby Getaways

Edinburgh folk are incredibly fond of their city, but they're just as much in love with their country. There are so many options for fun day trips from the city centre, so off you pop and haste ye back.

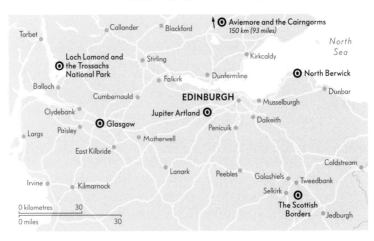

JUPITER ARTLAND

30-minute bus from city centre; www.jupiterartland.org

If you like your sculptures oversized and your views far-stretching, this 40-hectare (100-acre) immersive sculpture garden is the place for you. Jupiter Artland is home to some of the most impressive landscape design in the country. While the sweeping grounds are an artwork in themselves (and the perfect backdrop for some stunning snaps), they're also dotted with quirky sculptures and art installations.

GLASGOW

45-minute train from Edinburgh Waverley; www.peoplemakeglasgow.com

Ask any weegie for the best thing to do in Edinburgh and they'll direct you to the next train to Glasgow. Whether they're right or not remains a point of contention between the two rival cities, but we have to admit Glasgow is Edinburgh's bigger, edgier and, dare we say it, cooler older sibling. Experience the city through its street art on the Glasgow Mural Trail, catch a gig at legendary music venue Barrowland Ballroom and hit up Hillhead Book Club for a slap-up supper and ping-pong party.

» Don't leave without picking up some serious bargains at the Barras – a busy weekend street market in Glasgow's East End.

THE SCOTTISH BORDERS

1-hour train from Edinburgh Waverley

Edinburgers seeking a rural fix hop on a train to the charming town of Tweedbank – the perfect base for exploring the Scottish Borders. From here they stroll along the pretty riverside path to Abbotsford, Sir Walter Scott's stately home. Others hike the nearby Eildon Hills that overlook the town or head to Glentress Forest for some world-class mountain biking. Come the end of the day you'll find one and all congregating at Tempest Brewery to enjoy a pint while they wait for the train home. Ask for head brewer Big Hodge, he'll sort you out.

Liked by the locals

"Edinburgh is the perfect base for onward adventures. Whether it's sailing on the West Coast, camping in the Highlands or an evening stroll along the East Coast's beaches, the diversity of activities available to us right on our doorstep is really second to none."

PUNIT DESAI, OUTDOOR ENTHUSIAST

NORTH BERWICK

30-minute train from Edinburgh Waverley; www.north-berwick.co.uk

City slickers seeking some sea air make a beeline for this old-fashioned Victorian seaside resort. Yes, there are sandy beaches, but the town itself is a pretty cool place, packed with quirky boutiques, art galleries, kitsch coffee shops (hello, Steampunk) and sublime sea food. Locals don't even mind queuing for lunch from the legendary Lobster Shack.

» Don't leave without sampling award-winning gelato in more flavours than you knew existed at Alandas Gelateria. Charcoal, anyone?

LOCH LOMOND AND THE TROSSACHS NATIONAL PARK

1 hour 30 minutes' drive from city centre; www.lochlomond-trossachs.org

There may not be a monster in these waters, but with the towering peak of Ben Lomond standing tall as a backdrop, it's no wonder Loch Lomond has the heart of so many Scots. Those who don't fancy bagging a Munro make their way up the slightly more manageable Conic Hill for some epic views across the loch.

AVIEMORE AND THE CAIRNGORMS

3-hour train from Edinburgh Waverley; www.visitaviemore.com

Aviemore may not be a looker, but this wee town is a busy hub for adventurers seeking their next mountain fix, whether that involves hiking up challenging trails in summer or hurtling themselves down snowy slopes in winter. Either way, the reward is usually dinner at Macduis and a local brew from the Cairngorm Brewery.

An afternoon by the sea in
Portobello

The people of Edinburgh have been making the short trip from the city centre to enjoy the bright lights and pleasure pier of this Victorian resort for generations. Its popularity fell with the rise of package holidays, and the once busy resort town is now a peaceful escape offering sea air and coastal views. Dog walkers meander along the sand, couples stroll hand in hand and intrepid swimmers take to the chilly water no matter what time of year.

1. Nobles Amusements
47–9 Figgate Lane;
0131 669 8418;
///strain.thanks.voice

2. The Espy
62–4 Bath Street;
0131 669 0082;
///sums.slides.maple

3. Have a Dook
Wherever you fancy, but we think this spot is pretty sweet:
///hill.slips.urgent

4. Beer Zoo
219 Portobello High Street;
www.shop.beerzoo.co.uk;
///proper.closet.august

5. St Andrews Restaurant
280–84 Portobello High Street; www.standrews takeaway.co.uk;
///clean.free.melon

6. Enjoy the view
Portobello Promenade;
///dock.drips.major

Peddling local food and crafts, **Portobello Local Market** *is held in Brighton Park on the first Saturday of every month.*

📍 **Big Beach Busk** ///stick.mats.plug
📍 **Portobello Local Market** ///commented.towns.lovely

PROMENADE

PORTOBELLO HIGH STREET

SIR HARRY

Hit up
NOBLES AMUSEMENTS

Few folk can remember a time before Nobles. Indulge in some retro kitsch fun at this family-run arcade.

On the last Saturday of August musicians and buskers perform on Portobello Promenade for Edinburgh's **Big Beach Busk**.

1

Portobello Beach

Brave the cold and
HAVE A DOOK

Go open-water swimming with self-proclaimed eejits the Wild Ones. Join the Facebook group for details or go it alone.

2

PROMENADE

Straiton Place Park

Chill out at
THE ESPY

Nab an outdoor table at this beachfront pub and sip some of its famous home-brewed, alcohol-free ginger beer as you watch the world go by.

3

Portobello Beach

EIGGATE ST

Swing by
BEER ZOO

Time to pick up some mouthwatering speciality brews from every Edinburgh beer lover's favourite shop, Beer Zoo.

SHTON PLACE

4

PORTOBELLO

BELLFIELD STREET

Pick a bench and
ENJOY THE VIEW

Stroll back towards the water and find yourself a spot to sit and enjoy your fish supper with a sea view. A match made in heaven.

6

JOHN STREET

5

Grab a takeaway at
ST ANDREWS RESTAURANT

No visit to the seaside is complete without fish 'n' chips, so head over to St Andrews on the High Street and get yourself a fresh fish supper to go.

PORTOBELLO HIGH STREET

Abercorn Park

ABERCORN TERRACE

UDER ROAD

Firth of Forth

0 metres 250
0 yards 250

With a little research and preparation, this city will feel like a home away from home. Check out these websites to ensure a healthy, safe stay in Edinburgh.

Edinburgh
DIRECTORY

SAFE SPACES

Edinburgh is a friendly and inclusive city, but should you feel uneasy or want to find your community, there's a host of spaces catering to different genders, sexualities, demographics and religions.

www.edmosque.org
Edinburgh Central Mosque, the city's main mosque and Islamic cultural centre.

www.ehcong.com
The Edinburgh Hebrew Congregation, a welcoming Jewish community group.

www.lgbthealth.org.uk
Runs the LGBT Helpline Scotland and offers useful information and support.

www.scorescotland.org.uk
An organization serving and supporting minority ethnic communities in Edinburgh.

HEALTH

Healthcare in the UK is free for UK residents and holders of a European Health Insurance Card (EHIC). Visitors from elsewhere may need to pay for medical expenses upfront, so it's worth having insurance. If you need medical assistance, there are clinics, pharmacies and hospitals across town.

www.boots.com
Popular UK-wide pharmacy chain open daily with multiple branches in town.

www.breathingspace.scot
A free, confidential phone and web service for people experiencing depression or anxiety.

www.edinburghcrisiscentre.org.uk
Scotland's first mental health crisis centre, including a 24-hour helpline.

www.lothiansexualhealth.scot
Local provider of sexual health services with information on sexual health clinics.

www.nhs24.scot
NHS non-emergency helpline providing urgent medical advice day and night.

www.nhslothian.scot
Information on emergency dental care and local hospitals, including the Royal Infirmary, the only hospital in the city with a 24-hour A&E department.

TRAVEL SAFETY ADVICE

Edinburgh is generally a safe city. Before you travel – and while you're here – always keep tabs on the latest regulations in Scotland.

www.gov.scot
The official Scottish government website, the first port of call for all COVID-19 restrictions in place in Scotland.

www.lothianbuses.com/accessibility
Safety and accessibility information plus timetables and updates on city buses and trams from the Lothian Bus service.

www.scotland.police.uk
Useful information about major police incidents in the city.

ACCESSIBILITY

Edinburgh has come on in leaps and bounds when it comes to accessibility, but some of its medieval streets and old infrastructure can prove tricky for wheelchair users. Here are some useful websites and resources.

www.disabilityrightsuk.org
The National Key Scheme offers disabled people access to locked public toilets.

www.edinburgh.org
A great resource on all things Edinburgh, with specific information and handy tips for travellers with specific requirements.

www.euansguide.com
A forum founded in Edinburgh for disabled access, featuring reviews on restaurants, theatres and attractions by and for people with specific requirements.

www.relayuk.bt.com
App that helps those who are hearing- or speech-impaired to contact 999 (emergency services) via SMS.

www.visitscotland.com
Tourist board website with the latest advice and useful information on accessible accommodation for travellers with specific requirements.

ABOUT THE ILLUSTRATOR

Mantas Tumosa

Creative designer and illustrator Mantas moved from his home country of Lithuania to London back in 2011. By day, he's busy creating bold, minimalistic illustrations that tell a story – such as the gorgeous cover of this book. By night, he's dreaming of adventures away, catching up on the basketball and cooking Italian food (which he can't get enough of).

Main Contributors Kenza Marland, Michael Clark, Stuart Kenny, Xandra Robinson-Burns

Senior Editor Lucy Richards

Senior Designer Tania Gomes

Project Editor Danielle Watt

Project Art Editor Bandana Paul

Editor Rachel Laidler

Proofreader Stephanie Smith

Senior Cartographic Editor Casper Morris

Cartography Manager Suresh Kumar

Cartographer Ashif

Jacket Designer Tania Gomes

Jacket Illustrator Mantas Tumosa

Senior Production Editor Jason Little

Senior Production Controller Stephanie McConnell

Managing Editor Hollie Teague

Managing Art Editor Bess Daly

Art Director Maxine Pedliham

Publishing Director Georgina Dee

First edition 2022

Published in Great Britain by Dorling Kindersley Limited,
DK, One Embassy Gardens, 8 Viaduct Gardens,
London SW11 7BW.

The authorised representative in the EEA is
Dorling Kindersley Verlag GmbH. Arnulfstr. 124,
80636 Munich, Germany.

Published in the United States by DK Publishing,
1745 Broadway, New York, NY 10019.

Copyright © 2022 Dorling Kindersley Limited
A Penguin Random House Company
23 24 25 10 9 8 7 6 5 4 3

A CIP catalog record for this book is available from the British Library.

A catalog record for this book is available from the Library of Congress.

ISSN: 1542 1554
ISBN: 978 0 2415 2388 9

Printed and bound in China.

www.dk.com

A NOTE FROM DK EYEWITNESS

The world is fast-changing and it's keeping us folk at DK Eyewitness on our toes. We've worked hard to ensure that this edition of Edinburgh Like a Local is up-to-date and reflects today's favourite places but we know that standards shift, venues close and new ones pop up in their place. So, if you notice something has closed, we've got something wrong or left something out, we want to hear about it. Please drop us a line at travelguides@dk.com